# Stories

# From

# Heaven

## Volume XXIV

# STORIES FROM HEAVEN®
Copyright © 1996 FMK

First printing 2002
Volume XXIV
ISBN 1-892957-24-8
Printed in the United States of America

Published By:
The City Of God
Saint Joseph's Hill Of Hope
Post Office Box 1055
Brea, California 92822


www.TheMiracleOfStJoseph.Org

# PREFACE

These "Stories From Heaven" could not have been given to the world at a more appropriate time than now.  The world is in a terrible state of corruption and confusion politically, religiously and socially.  Honesty, modesty, genteelness and morality seem to have been eliminated from our way of life, at least in effect if not consciously.  However, God has given the world a Miracle it needs.

On July 28, 1967 The Miracle Of Saint Joseph was formally announced to a True Mystic. God has chosen a woman to give us the sound direction, hope and example we need.  It is not the first time God has chosen a woman to accomplish His Purpose, always for a specific task in a . particular time.  This True Mystic for our day is Frances Marie Klug.  She resides in Southern California and is a wife, a mother, and a grandmother.

In this Miracle Of Saint Joseph, many Saints have come forth to speak through Frances Klug.  These "Stories From Heaven" are just a few of the thousands of Revelations received through her.  Very often these Revelations were preceded by extensive Teachings which time and space did not allow us to put in print.  However, a few of these Teachings will be found in one of the succeeding Volumes of "Stories From Heaven".

In these Revelations the Saints refer to Frances as the "child", the "funnel", the "spoon" and the "instrument". God made her our Spiritual Mother. For many years now, because of this fact, she has been called "Mother Frances", or simply "Mother". Heaven also refers to people of all ages as "children" and emphasizes time and again, this Miracle is for people of all races, all colors and all creeds.

For someone turning the pages of these "Stories From Heaven" for the first time, they will easily recognize the sound logic and sound direction the Messages contain. Mother Frances hears the Words with the ears of her Soul, and repeats them aloud when she is told to do so.

This Teaching Miracle is a direct parallel to the time Our Lord walked the earth. He did not loudly proclaim to everyone, "I am The Son of God." He taught in a quiet manner, simple, extensive, but always detailed in repetitiveness, instilling in those listening what He wanted them to remember. He taught in parables, short, simple stories containing moral lessons. He knew men could more easily understand and remember the point He was trying to make this way. His "teaching stories" pertained to everyday living, practical matters, and how to become a Saint. He gave hope through these stories. He gave example.

Now in our time, God is once again giving us "teaching stories" through Saint Joseph and His instrument, Mother Frances. Through her, in a quiet, unassuming and genteel way which appears so "natural", mankind is again being taught the purpose of life, and what God expects man to be like in his daily living. People feel hope in these Teachings. Example is being given.

Two major Revelations of significance have been given for us in our day. Our Heavenly Mother is Part of The Divine, and Saint Joseph is truly The Holy Ghost. These should not bring an immediate rejection, but should pique our curiosity and interest.

Our Faith in God is based upon many mysteries. Whether it be The Holy Trinity, the Incarnation of God, or the Holy Eucharist, men strive to understand these, trying to grasp a small glimpse of the beauty of the Truth They Are. These mysteries also pique our imagination and interest. However, even though we know God revealed these mysteries to mankind and we accept them in faith, they still remain just that, mysteries.

One has only to look at these "Stories From Heaven" to see the value they are, and to feel the hope they instill. No man can logically deny purity of thought when it is so obvious. No man can deny purity in direction, when it is based on sound morals, sound values, sound standards. Do not be blind to truth. Skepticism is for people who are unable to see the truth of a matter or situation, and many times skepticism drowns out purity because it is full of ego and pride in one's self. Skeptics find it an easy out to disclaim truth.

There is no doubt that it takes time for such Phenomena as this Miracle to penetrate even those minds who feel they are capable of discerning such phenomena. We must not be governed by purely another man's determination, but we must understand that logic, sound reasoning and purpose must be the criteria of our Faith in God.

*Stories From Heaven*

All Revelations are delivered
spontaneously and continuously
as witnessed by all those present
at the time.

*Stories From Heaven*

OCTOBER 30, 2001 AT 12:23 P.M.

### SAINT DOMINIC

"**I** am Saint Dominic.  It has been some time since I have come to speak through this Gift of The Father's Love that is a Gift beyond what mankind can imagine It to be.

**W**hen a human being receives something of great worth, whether it be monetary, jewelry, or a trip around the world, it is always thought about as being the ultimate gift the human being can receive.

*Today as I speak, I have come to make you all aware, all who read these Words, that the Greatest Gift that a human being can recognize as being the Ultimate Gift is the understanding that each human being is born with a Soul, a Portion of The Creator that nothing else has.* The Soul, though It is not seen, is innately felt in many ways, when an individual has the insight, the understanding to realize that an act or action is either pure or impure, just or unjust, right or wrong.

There are so many *excuses* made by all ages, and they are only *excuses*, avoiding the Importance of the Soul they are the custodian of, thus accepting something that can, in many ways, disgrace the Soul or cause impurity to the Soul, that reparation will have to be made.  It is sad for so Many of Us

Here in the Heavens Who see The Father
giving to the world so much Information
through the ability for human beings to write
What is spoken, so they will not forget the
Importance of the Subject Matter.

*The Soul can be a victim so easily
through the one in whom It was placed at
the moment of conception, ignoring the
Magnitude of What they have been given
to give them Strength, Honor, and a
Closeness to The Creator that nothing
else is the custodian of, but also, when
the physical no longer exists the Soul
never dies.* It always represents the one in
whom It was placed, but the Soul becomes the
victim of disgrace, and pays for what the
individual did immorally, impurely, unjustly.

The Soul, as a Gift of Divine Love, is
the Protector during one's lifetime. The Soul
aids the individual in more fully
understanding right over wrong, purity over
impurity, justice over injustice, kindness over
hate.

As I close, I plead with those who write
these Words to see that They are distributed
far and wide, and not worry about Them being
rejected, because truth has a way of saving
Souls, and truth binds one's whole being to
the value of life because of the Soul that, each
day of an individual's life, works very hard to
help the individual in whom It was placed at
the moment of conception, to value purity of
the mind and the body over impurities, justice

over injustices, and love over hate, but so many individuals become so aware of humanistic values that they ignore the importance of what is right, what is pure, what is logical, and what would please The Creator.

Even when someone ignores the fact that there is, and always has been, a Divine Entity of Creation, Creating All Things, there is an innate sensitivity, but sometimes the enemy of The Father and man uses a weakness for the wrong things to be said, done, or practiced.

As I close, I beseech you, never delay or stop All that has been delivered through this Gift of Divine Love, because the Souls of millions of human beings will be helped by what you have accepted the responsibility of."

NOVEMBER 5, 2001 AT 12:44 P.M.

## OUR HEAVENLY FATHER

"**I** am your Heavenly Father.  I am The Creator, I Am The One Who will Judge you — your Soul — at a given time.

I created human life for a Great Purpose.  I gave to human life portions of being able to be likened to Me in some ways — the ability to think, to have a memory, and to do many other things.

As I have blessed so many individuals through time, I have blessed the whole world this time, with My Will for Many Saints Here with Me to speak, leave Words of Guidance, Hope, to be cherished, helping human life fully understand the importance of being made man, but also, that there is a Goal for the Soul of human life that nothing else possesses, nothing else can have.

The Soul is That Portion to be returned to Where I Am, the Heavenly Way of Living in My Divine Plan.

I could speak hours on My Love for human life, and the importance for which I created it, but today I will shorten My Words, because of the 'preparation' I have just allowed to be on this little instrument of Mine, to be able to give more strength to more men, women and children at given times.

My Statement will be difficult for many to understand, but the little one through whom I pass so much through, is aware of the Purpose, the Reason for this 'preparation' she must endure.

Be example to all you meet, be example to all you love, because in doing this the Soul is the recipient, even when the physical appears as though nothing occurred, nothing was said.

I beseech you to remember that human life has a Goal. It is worth everything you do to give hope, and to show the importance of human life, and that you believe that a Portion of yourself, and others, will one day return to Me and be called Saints.

Remember, your life has a Goal, and also remember, It Is Sainthood For Your Soul. So be it."

NOVEMBER 6, 2001 AT 12:30 P.M.

### SAINT ATHANASIUS

"**I** am Saint Athanasius.

You live in a time in which many heresies are prevalent, and practiced daily throughout the world. There are so many excuses for why individuals make choices that are logically wrong, regarding the category of sound religious beliefs, sound understanding of a Divine Creator, and that Souls become Saints.

*The world has been blessed with this Gift of The Beloved Saint Joseph, because as The Holy Spirit of The Creator, He has come to the world at this time, not just to enlighten human beings of all ages, backgrounds or understanding, but to instruct them on the importance of human life, and that it was created to one day return to The Father for All Time.*

That Portion of human life is unseen, but That Portion of human life will one day be called by the name of the one in whom It was placed in the human way, but It will be judged on what the individual practiced morally on every issue; also, how many times that the wrong decision was made due to some foolish thought, or trying to please someone else's opinion.

The Father has given to the world a Miracle of Great Dimension to enlighten all of mankind. *Not just one religion, but every human being born should understand that, as a Creation of The Divine, they should use all they are to return to The Creator of All That Portion called the Soul.*

It is so easy for All of Us Saints to speak about, and it is a privilege because in All that We speak, Each of Us does it in a little different way, hoping to touch millions of individuals through the wording We use, to draw their attention to the fact that to walk the human way was a privilege; and then one day, to have an individual's Soul return to The Creator a Saint, is beyond what the human mind can fully understand or comprehend, but It Is Fact.

Scientists never find the answer they want when they first approach a project, a subject.

Human life has been given, in so many ways, the importance of human life, the reasons for which it should be handled in a pure way. No excuse can be made for a sinful act, a vile contemptible disgrace to one's Soul.

*All of the Saints Here in the Heavens plead through this Miracle, to be aware that human life has a Goal, and It is Far Greater than any goal in the human way, because the Soul, as a*

*Portion of The Creator, is the Greatest Gift of Divine Love, and each individual has the privilege of returning It to The Creator, a Saint.* So be it."

NOVEMBER 7, 2001 AT 12:43 P.M.

SAINT ATHANASIUS

"**I** am Saint Athanasius.

**C**hildren are not being instructed on what is moral, what is immoral. It is important that all ages should understand that there is a reason for human life. It has a Goal.

**W**e hear some say: 'What makes me think I have a Goal?' I say to them: 'Do you not always look at a situation, a condition, or the value of something, innately looking for the goal for which it was instituted, created, or set in a definite value higher than something else, maybe a lot of other things, not just one thing?'

**I**n the creation of human life, The Father, in His Love for this Gift of His Divine Love, gave a Goal to the intellect. The Goal was greater than the early men, women and children fully realized it to be. *That is why Christ Himself had to come to the earth and openly Speak, Instruct that within human life there was a Purpose, and that human life was designed to reach for a Goal.*

**M**any understood it to be a material thing, a physical matter, until they were instructed openly, lovingly, that as long as they realized what a Goal meant, they should see it for the Goal within them, because they were innately given the realization, the practicality, the reasonability that human life had a Goal, and it was a Goal Far Greater than what human life offered in earthly measures.

**When The Son of The Creator was put upon the earth, He Instructed constantly on the Purpose for which human life was created.** A lot of men, women and children felt the In-depth Love, and understood the practicality of this Message, the reasonability of It, the logic.

The world has been blessed many times by The One Who created it, and each era of time was instructed in a lengthier description of the importance of human life.

We hear men, women and children put much emphasis on Bible History. That is good, because Bible History gave a foundation understandable to many things. It is true, the mentality of human life at this time now in which you live, has grown in many directions, supposedly elevated to almost a brilliance on many subjects, giving subjects great attention and more feasibility in being involved in them.

I do not say this is wrong, but I do say one thing: So many human beings of all backgrounds are ignoring why human life was created. Some have become extremely interested in their version, ignoring what was told a long time ago, *that Sainthood should be the Goal, thus meaning, returning the Soul to The Creator from Where It came; but it is to be remembered, It was given in a Pure State, and It must be returned in a Pure State.*

I hear some say: 'How will I know what a Pure State is? I live an ordinary life.' This statement is logical, but *the Commandments of The Creator were given to give the Directions to be followed by all of human life*. There is a sadness on part of this one portion of it. What was truly and fully delivered has been for a long time shortened to a point of one word being the important point of understanding the *'full meaning'* of the Commandment.

To speak all the hours I could, on this Important Subject, would be difficult to take at this time, but hopefully, What I have spoken will awaken thousands and thousands of minds to the Reality, the Purpose, the Reasoning in each Commandment, because it will give strength to how one talks, how one plans things, how one associates with others like themselves, human beings; *also, how much guidance will be given to children of all ages so they will understand that to be born a human being is a Blessing of Divine Love that nothing else is gifted with.*

As I leave you, I want to say one thing: If you make it a habit to silently say, when you are parting from someone you have been

with, you have talked with, or you even had
something very important to deal with, say to
yourself, not so it can be heard, *'God Bless
you'."*

NOVEMBER 8, 2001 AT 12:38 P.M.


## SAINT ALPHONSUS LIGUORI

"**I** am Saint Alphonsus Liguori.

**A**ll of what has passed through this Gift of Divine Love must be transmitted throughout the world in languages understandable to millions of human life.

**M**en, women and children are starving in the physical way, but they are also starving in their love for God. There is so little logic, in a spiritual form, being transmitted in areas wherein thousands of individuals live.

**T**oday, as All of the Saints speak through this Gift of The Father's Love, so little is being transmitted to the degree to cover all areas of human life.

**A**s I speak today, I speak differently, but I have come to enlighten you, to inform you, and to request of you that All that has been delivered through this Gift of Divine Love never be held in one place, but be spread throughout the world. It is needed more than you can conceive It to be needed.

**T**hose who are close to this Gift are aware of the Greatness of It, in It, for It. It is time that It be transmitted in languages understandable to those who cannot be present where you are. So be it."

NOVEMBER 9, 2001 AT 12:43 P.M.

## OUR HEAVENLY MOTHER

"I am your Heavenly Mother.

Wherever this little one is, The Father uses her to communicate, for All of Us Here in the Heavens, subjects important to the Souls, the bodies, and the mentalities of all ages of human life.

Morality has been dismissed as a category of what life practices. Morality has turned into many obscenities of the mind and the flesh. Too little is being instructed to the young on the importance of their actions, their thoughts, their moods, their intentions, their weaknesses and, of course, their strengths.

So much is allowed to be spoken, that if it were not spoken, immorality would not be as open as it is, and has been. It is more important that children of all ages learn that the subject matter they become involved in should be of a higher level; also, interesting to think about, to act upon, to give hope and more understanding of the beauty of human life.

Many Saints Here in the Heavens listen to thousands of words every day, and when I say 'day', this includes the twenty-four hours that human life is capable of using, in many ways.

The world has become like it was a long time ago, resisting what is pure, rejecting the fact that foul language, foul actions cause the Soul great harm. So little is instructed on that Portion of human life that is unseen by the human eye, but obviously present, because of an individual's abilities to express knowingly, words, subjects, ideas, that pertain to a Portion of themselves, more fully understanding, or expressing what is pure, what is impure, what is just, what is unjust.

The Father has given to the world, the whole world, this Gift of His Divine Love that bears the Name of The Beloved Saint Joseph. Saint Joseph, in life, appeared ordinary to the human eye, as Our Lady did in the Purpose for which She was put upon the earth visibly.

As I speak today, I speak with Deep Love, and yet great concern for the whole world of human life. Too much is occurring that pleases only the enemy, ignoring The Creator, and of course, damaging the Soul in more ways than would be discernible to the human mind.

As I leave you, I plead with you: Do not ignore the Goal for which you were Created, because your Soul pleads constantly for the one in whom It is, to be more pure in thoughts, actions, example, deeds.

As I leave you today, always remember, I am as close to you as I am your whole being. These Words may be difficult for some to understand, but all they need to do is speak in a silent manner, because the Soul is constantly aware of Our Presence, and also in all you do. So be it."

NOVEMBER 9, 2001 AT 1:15 P.M.

## SAINT THERESE OF LISIEUX

"**I** am Saint Therese of Lisieux. Many of Us Saints were present the night this Gift was Announced to this one small body. As We put her in what you call 'ecstasy', We protected her when she left where she had to come to be told she had been chosen for a 'special' way of life. As she drove, she does not remember the drive. We were in control of the automobile at all times.

The moment of 'preparation' was not easy; it never is, but all the 'preparations' that must be experienced takes a toll on the intellect and the physical, in ways unknown to the human mind of those who are present; also, when We speak.

You have been blessed to be present each time you have been able to hear the Words pour forth through her from One Here. All the Saints discuss this Gift in many ways, because this Particular Gift, in which The Beloved Saint Joseph is the Main One Who is Honored and Revered, *The Father, at this time, decided that the world must more fully understand the Greatness of The Beloved Saint Joseph and how Important He Was and Is, in Divine Plan.*

The world must see this Miracle, hear about It, and read about It, because It is a Gift of Divine Love at a time when human life of all ages, backgrounds, degrees of intellect, must more fully understand that there is a Heaven, there is a Purgatory, there is a Hell, *and that human life was created with a Portion of The Creator, giving human life a special role, different than anything else created by The Creator of All Things.*

So many men, women and children study what they call 'theology', oftentimes ignoring the reality of how close they are to where The Father works in their midst, helping them to better understand, to more fully be able to comprehend, what a privilege it is to be born the human way called 'man'.

As I close My Words with those here with Me at this time, I want you to remember: *Human life has a Purpose, a Goal, a Plan, and human life is Gifted Higher than any other living matter or thing. Use each day in a way that will help you grow closer to more fully understand that your Soul is a Portion of The Creator, and truly a Gift beyond any gift the human way could give or plan.* So be it."

NOVEMBER 12, 2001 AT 12:43 P.M.

## OUR HEAVENLY MOTHER

"**I** am your Heavenly Mother. As I speak to you today there are Several Who stand with Me, listening to everything I say.

The world has been blessed by this Gift of The Father's Love, allowing so much to be spoken openly, consistently, with a Purpose that, for some, it is difficult to understand, but if they look at the logic in the meaning of All that is spoken, they will see that it was not delivered by man.

Children throughout the world, all ages, are in need of All the Words that have passed through this Gift of Divine Love. It is sad when We see some men, women and children ignore this Gift, and buy script that is harmful to their minds, their way of life, and definitely their Souls. We hear some individuals say, 'There is a price on what I buy, so it must be good.'

Today as I speak through one small voice there is no price to pay for the Love that I express in speaking Words of Direction, of Hope. The Will of The Father is to have all Souls return to Him in a State of Purity, so when They return to Him there will be no place before Him that They will have to go, to repent for sins of the flesh, the mind, and also the sins that they caused others to take part in.

I hold the little one tightly, because I come in a very strong way today. There is so much that has been given through this Gift of Divine Love, not only for the Souls, but the importance of human life, instructing that human life has a Goal, and that each Soul that is returned to The Father has a name, the name They bore in the human way.

Children are being allowed impurities of the mind and the body, with those in charge of them saying, 'It is because they are human beings, and it is part of human life to act this way.' There have been many times in the history of human life that wrong has been accepted, right has been ignored, and truth was passed off as being for another time.

As I hold this little one through whom I speak, and she responds to My Words so you will have My Words to remember the importance of human life, and that millions of human beings, all ages, all degrees of intellect learn about this Gift of The Father's Love.

True, the Gift was blessed with the Name of The Beloved Saint Joseph, for do not forget, in reality, He is The Holy Spirit of The Creator of All Things, which makes this Gift Bearing His Name More Important than the average human being sees It to be, for The Father Himself passes through His Own Holy Spirit, Instructing all of human life, and allowing All the Saints Here in the Heavens to participate in this Great Gift that is now taking place in your time.

As We watch and hear some with the Words that have thus far been delivered in Our Own Way, We encourage them to believe What they have read that has been written for them to read, because human life is special.

We hear some say, 'I prayed to Saint ...', and they mention a Name. They should then ask themselves: 'How did They become a Saint? They lived a human life before that time They were given that title "Saint".'

There are so many throughout the world, men, women and even children, who claim to believe in The Creator of All Things, but they do not act the part, and they ignore the Rules, thus making the Rules no foundation for how they live, how they think, how they talk, how they act.

So much Divine Love is in each time One of Us speaks. It is Greater in Value than anyone can perceive, because to have It so Immediate, so Direct, gives more of a Personal Feeling to Our Presence in you, around you, for you.

I beseech you, remember this: As I stand Here and speak to you, the Saints Who surround Me are great in number, and Each One of Them prays in Their own way, with Their own words, that The Father will give you the strength, and all who read these Words, to one day join Them.

We hear some say: 'What is a Soul? I cannot see It, I cannot feel It.' The Soul is a Portion of The Creator, and It should never be mistaken for anything else. It is impossible for human life to fully understand What The Father of all life is like, the Greatness of What He Is, but always keep in mind the logic that there is, and has to be, a Higher Being in Existence, else there would be nothing on earth to give credence to how things occur, or how human life began. The list is endless.

I bless you with a Mother's Love, and I plead with you, be example of all that is pure, because your Soul is the recipient of what you are, what you do, and what example you portray to help others become Saints.

As I bless you with My Love, I bless you with the courage to follow The Father's Will that you become a Saint."

NOVEMBER 13, 2001 AT 12:40 P.M.

SAINT PEREGRINE

"**I** am Saint Peregrine.

**I**t is unbelievable to many who read All that has been delivered through this Gift of Divine Love. Some say, 'How could anyone speak so many times, in so many ways, unless it was truly Someone using their voice, their mind, to deliver the Important Subjects that seem so easy to understand when They are dictated, put into script, and to be handed out to all of mankind.'

**T**he Father, in giving this Gift in the manner and way He does, is because the Written Word will remain longer than anything said verbally, or spoken repetitively.

**I** smile at the little one through whom I speak, because she stares at My Face. What she sees is not as a statue, but as a Light, different than any other light could be.

*The Father has given, at this time, so much Love for His Creation, human life. Millions of Words have been spoken over the years, even before this Gift of The Father's Love was Formally Announced to mankind.*

**T**here is so much dissension amongst many who feel they have the ability to instruct on The Divine. There are other words that can also describe what many of them feel. To some, it is almost a disinterest; to some, it is a repetitiveness of what they have learned; and to many, there is very little sensitivity to the meaning that must be expressed, regarding what human life possesses, *and that is a Portion of The Creator, and This should never be scandalized or blemished in any way.*

There is so little instruction on the importance of human life and the Goal for which it was created. So much of human life is taken for granted, but done in such obvious, incredible versions of its purpose.

The Father has given a Special Gift through one voice. Some might say, 'Why one voice?' I smile when I say the next words: 'If there were many voices at one time, would not it cause a lot of confusion?'

*This Gift that bears the Name of The Beloved Holy Saint Joseph, has addressed so many Important Subjects, instructing all degrees of intellect on the Importance of human creation, its Purpose, its Goal.*

The world is in desperate need of All that has been delivered, put into print, for the souls that are starving to know what they were created for, and that there truly exists within them, more than what they see, what they feel, as human life.

Prayer has dwindled in many ways, in all ages. I cannot understand this, nor can any Other Saints Here in the Heavens understand this, because prayer is a communication.

Some say, 'I hear nothing back. Maybe that is why I do not pray more often.' These words are only excuses. Ask yourself, 'How many times have I had a conversation with all types of people and received no responses?' Why? Because they were too busy discerning the full meaning of what was spoken, or they felt it did not apply to them.

There are multiple reasons, too many to speak of now, but no prayer goes unheard, though this may be difficult for some to understand; but The Father has made communication with The Divine different than any other communication. Everything that is spoken is heard. Everything that is thought is visible. Every intention is seen, in a way, a degree, a manner, that would be difficult to explain in words at this time, but as each Saint speaks, We do it. It is the Will of The Father to awaken the minds of human beings of all degrees of intellect, all natures, that there is a Goal to human life for a Portion of them that is also a Portion of The Creator — a Soul.

When We hear individuals say, 'We are soul mates to each other,' Our Words are not heard, but We respond in a manner and way, trying to enlighten the individual to understand that as you feel the responsibility of being a soul mate to someone else, *it is important you remember that your Soul is a Portion of The Creator, and what you have in mind can only compare to a very minute degree, to the Magnitude of What one's Soul Is, in reality.*

*As I leave you, please remember: There is time to use all you are, and all you need to change within you, to make your Goal 'Sainthood'."*

NOVEMBER 14, 2001 AT 12:30 P.M.


SAINT ATHANASIUS

"**I** am Saint Athanasius.

**T**here are many heresies being practiced in all parts of the world. Many so-called learned men and women are attracted to heresies because they feel it expands their thinking in areas they would not have thought advisable at another time.

**C**hildren are not being instructed on the basics of what is moral, what is immoral, what is just, what is unjust; thus, this type of teaching or lack of teaching can allow little understanding of what is moral, what is immoral.

**F**ew individuals ever think of the Soul they are the custodian of. To some It's a myth. To some It's imagination. To some It is something that was talked about in the early years. But I assure you, human beings were gifted with a Soul, a Portion of The Creator; difficult for some to understand, but it is logical for an individual to realize evidence of all that has been created, no human being could do.

*So then, this Gift of The Father's Love, this Miracle that instructs on so many subjects, for the purpose of the Souls of millions of human beings, must be seen for the Truths that pour forth*

***from It and the Instructions that are
constant, even in what is called natural
speech.***

As I leave you, those who are taking My
Words in print, I beseech you to see that the
whole world receives All that The Father has
directed and allowed to be delivered, because
of the importance of human life and that
Portion of Him that is within it. So be it."

NOVEMBER 15, 2001 AT 12:48 P.M.


### SAINT CATHERINE OF SIENA

"**I** am Saint Catherine of Siena. There are Many of Us present as We have All gathered to speak on a subject or subjects to give strength morally, mentally, physically, psychologically, to all degrees of intellects who will read the Words, or be told verbally What was spoken by Us at a specific time.

**W**e are gathered in a Group, and Each of Us smiles as the little one through whom We speak, searches for Our Faces which she cannot see. Her next statement to Us is a joy to Us, beyond what a human being will understand this joy to be. She says, 'I must be seeing Your Souls, so Your Souls are speaking to me.'

The Father, in His Love for this creation, human life, has instilled in it so many ways to understand what is right, what is wrong; also, the need for a desire to be happy over sadness, because sadness is difficult to handle emotionally, mentally, psychologically and physically.

The little one is staring at Us. What she sees is a fraction of what We truly look like.

*We have come to request that no area throughout the world is this Gift of Divine Love not to be seen, spoken about, making excuses for the language barrier.*

She stares at All of Us, and talks to Us with her mind. We smile at this, because her mental communication with Us is understandable to Us.

This is important for you to understand — those who read These Words — because oftentimes there is much more communication with All of Us Here in the Heavens, due to the mental communication that is available in thoughts regarding many issues, many facts, many ideas, that no one present on the earth can hear or sense in the reality it is occurring.

So many times men, women and children ignore the privilege they have of personal communication through their thoughts, their ideas, that they do not want to openly speak out so others hear.

We hold the little one tightly, and she is aware of a 'preparation' that has been occurring for some time now within her being.

Human life was created, and is created, to be accountable for a Portion of this privilege. It is called the 'Soul'. Think of it in this way: No one — man, woman or child — onjoys illness. It affects their whole being mentally, physically, emotionally, and all the senses of their body, their mind.

Ask yourself how many times you have said, 'When I get to church,' or 'When I get home,' or perhaps some other place, you connect prayer at a specific time. Perhaps at the moment you are thinking about this, you do not feel that it is the time to say what you want to say, because it is innate in you to feel that your communication with The Divine is separate and separated from your close association to other human beings.

*There is no time that you are without a Closeness to Every Saint Here in the Heavens. Your Soul is the Communicator, and then your mind.*

What I have spoken is different, but oh so logical. It is important that all of human life understand they are never a distance too great to talk to Anyone. *The Father Wills the Communication to be understood, that All of Heaven is available every moment of every day, and whether you are in a crowded room, or on a form of transportation that a lot of sound is coming from, it will never interfere with your Soul's Association, Closeness to The Divine.*

Children should be taught What I have just spoken, because sometimes all ages of human life feel the need to be in a special place to communicate their inner thoughts, their needs, their love, their hopes, their wishes. Do not forget, at the moment of conception, each human being is blessed with a Connecting Link to The Divine.

As I leave you, I want you to under-stand that you have been blessed in so many ways, to give you the strength for your own Soul, and to be example to other human beings so they will learn the practicality, the logic in the Gift of Divine Love, to be able to communicate momentarily at any given time.

As I leave you, I bless you with the strength to understand, ***human life has a Goal based on Divine Plan.*** So be it for now."

NOVEMBER 16, 2001 AT 12:45 P.M.

## OUR HEAVENLY MOTHER

"I am your Heavenly Mother. I smile as I say My next Words. There were so many Saints ready to speak and They saw Me enter, smiled and said, 'Holy Mother, will You please say the Words to help those who need What You have to say?'

If I were to list All the Saints that were waiting to speak, those who write these Words would have a page with no space on it, with so many Names.

It is important that this Gift of The Father's Love reach millions of human beings. There is so little understanding of what is wrong, what is right, what is impure, what is pure, and it is causing many sins against the flesh, the mental, the actions, and the understanding of all ages of human life.

I speak slowly through this little one. I smile when I say this, because she is concentrating on the Vision of My Presence. I will withdraw some so My Words will become more obvious to her.

The world has been blessed by The Father's Love for human life. Why is it then difficult for human beings of all backgrounds to understand the

importance of the responsibilities in
being a human being?

Human life is the only creation
that has been gifted with a mentality to
understand so many different things, so
much about many things, plus the ability
to value the importance of self-control
when it is needed, over how the enemy
would want a lack of self-control to be
what would be applied at a certain time,
to please him, drawing the individual
away from what would be rational, just,
kind and pleasing to The Father.

Some individuals, of all
backgrounds, cannot understand why
The Creator of All Things does not 'wipe
out' the evil one, the evil ones. This, of
course, is a human version of avoiding
the 'gift of choice' The Father has
instilled in the human mind.

Children must see good example
and be made aware that though they
have the 'gift of choice', it is wise for
them to choose what is pure, what is
just, over what is impure or unjust.

In the very beginning of human
life, those who were born used instinct
over what they understood, purity over
impurity, right over wrong.

I hold this little one deeply,
because as I speak, I show her the visual
situations of My Points that I express.

In the beginning of creation of human life, The Creator allowed one step at a time in advancement to what you have and what you are, in this time in which you live. Many of the Saints that were born in the physical role thousands of years ago, were given the chance, the responsibility, the knowledge to lay the groundwork for the millions that were yet to come.

All things created had a beginning. Perhaps you can compare it to the time in which you live: a new idea, a new advancement in some form, takes time to give it strength, purpose, reason. So it was, a long time ago.

Today as I speak, I speak with much Love for human life and desire only each human being to realize that they did not create themselves. They were created by a Supreme Power of Love, Justice.

In many places throughout the world, there is much diabolical interference, only because the enemy can use the weakness in individuals, encouraging them to use their minds in opposite manner, degrees, than what The Father Wills the minds to handle.

I know What I have spoken is different than Much that has been spoken before this time, but perhaps it is just to help you understand that as you live in a time that The Father has allowed so much progress to be understood, you will have the courage to stand strong on the value of things, whether these things be mental, moral, or just based on what the enemy would want, so that the Will of The Creator would not show.

I will close for now, for the Power I have used is beyond what the little one that We All use can endure much more of. So be it."

NOVEMBER 19, 2001 AT 12:54 P.M.

### SAINT ATHANASIUS

"**I** am Saint Athanasius.

There are many heresies being
practiced throughout the world.  They have
become so prevalent that they are being
accepted as what is called 'the norm' for men,
women and children — yes, even children —
to delight in what the heresies request them
to do, allow them to do, ignoring totally what
is morally sound, correct; also, what is
pleasing to The Creator.

*In so many ways the world has been
blessed with The Father's Love,* but it is
difficult for many who walk the human role to
see the value in what is morally sound, pure,
because in several generations down through
time now, immorality has become acceptable
in all ages, all backgrounds and all
nationalities.

So much has been delivered through
one small voice.  The meaning of What has
been spoken is so logical, factual,
understanding, but as We see individuals
reading the Words, We hear them say that
What they read does not seem to pertain to
them, because they feel their life is what they
call 'normal', and see no reason or necessity
to change how they think, how they act, how
they speak, how they associate what they call

'advancement in morals' when, in reality, it is not advancement, it is degrading in every facet they use. Immorality is prevalent throughout the world. *The Commandments of The Creator are totally ignored, even by many who have chosen the roles of spiritual instructors, leaders in Faith in The Divine.*

*As We All speak through one small voice, the Words are Important, because using one small voice eliminates confusion, also variations in opinions.*

I could speak hours on this subject, but What I have spoken thus far is to alert the human minds of millions of human beings to stop trusting in what is called 'up-to-date' or 'modern' in thinking, in actions, values and desires, because human life is as it was when it was first created. Time has not deviated from what is morally sound, morally pure, to what would be immoral, impure.

All of Us Saints Here in the Heavens love this Gift of The Father's Love, because We are allowed to speak openly, and knowing that it is put into script immediately, not waiting for someone's or a few individuals' minds to remember how they heard It, how they felt about It.

As I close My Words today, I beseech all who take the time to put into script What is spoken, to deliver All the Words that have thus far been given, and Any yet to come, pass

Them in languages throughout the world so
no Soul is left out.

    **I** offer you a prayer:

> *Heavenly Father, I beseech*
> *You to spread what You have*
> *taught me to spread — more*
> *love for You, more under-*
> *standing of Your Existence,*
> *and that human life has a*
> *Goal in Your Kingdom for*
> *their Soul."*

NOVEMBER 20, 2001 AT 12:41 P.M.

SEVERAL SAINTS

"**T**here is no time that there is just One Saint present where this Gift of Divine Love has been given at a time in which you live, because of the Importance of so many Souls that are in need of this Gift.

**W**e hear some say, 'Why does my Soul have to be present? I can hear.' We smile at this, because what the human mind expects hearing the Saints to be, is not a sound as the human voice is a sound. *That is why this Gift of Divine Love is so Important to the whole world of mankind. The Father has given through one voice, a Gift wherein All of the Saints can speak.* It is difficult for human beings to understand the human association with The Divine.

**I**f a Gift of hearing the Saints was given to all of human life, the distraction, the misinterpretations would be so numerous that it would be indefinable to describe the chaos that human beings would endure. *That is why, when a Gift of Divine Love is instilled in one human body, it is Important that All that must be revealed through the one voice, the one body, be put into script — All that is spoken — so that millions of human beings of all ages, all backgrounds, all degrees of intellect will be able to read the Important Words,*

***Directions that are necessary, for not just
the spiritual part of human life, but the
mental, the moral.***

  **T**his Gift that so much has been
delivered through is beyond human
understanding, but nonetheless It is a Gift
beyond what the human mind would
personally be able to do.

  **I** will make this very short.  The reason
I am making It short is because I am
answering questions that We hear regarding
this Gift that has been given to all of human
life, to better understand that The Father is
constantly aware, and constantly trying to
give strength where it is needed, hope where
it is needed, through the Soul of an
individual, or individuals who need it to grow
stronger spiritually, morally, and to help
them better understand that through their
Soul they have a communication as man,
every moment of the day.

  **M**y Words will be short, but I know
They will be Important to certain individuals
who will one day read Them, and better
understand, more fully comprehend, ***what a
Closeness The Creator is to man.***
So be it.”

NOVEMBER 21, 2001 AT 12:35 P.M.

There are Three Saints present: Saint Anne, Saint Clare; Our Lady is smiling. It's Our Blessed Mother, and Our Blessed Mother will talk.

## OUR BLESSED MOTHER

"**You live in a very important time, similar to the time My Son walked the earth — so much Beautiful Instruction, Direction, Care, being delivered to assist, to help, and to encourage all backgrounds in human lives, all talents and all abilities, to understand the beauty of truth.**

**The world, in many ways, has changed. Human beings of all backgrounds have allowed themselves to ignore important things, whether they be morals, wealth in many areas, not just financial wealth.**

**Today, as I speak through one small voice, it is important that this Gift of Divine Love, through which, and from which, so much Divine Love is shown, expressed, dealt with and delivered, encouraging all ages to understand that the Creation of human life was Special, is Special, because within it, it is given the opportunity to return a Portion of it.**

That Portion is a Portion of The Creator. It is called a Soul.

Animals don't have Souls, other types of creatures do not have Souls; they were all created for other reasons, but human life was created not just to the Image and Likeness, but for a Goal.

I have spoken to the little one a personal note of Our Love for this Gift that has placed so much responsibility within her, upon her. It has taken place a long time, this Gift of Divine Love, and it is important that all ages, all degrees of backgrounds become aware of this Blessing, that does not just encourage human beings to realize the importance of human life, but so much Instruction has been given, allowing the minds of so many to value the Information that, in many ways, binds human life to All The Saints.

Needless to say, I could speak hours on the Love that is generated through this Gift of The Father's Love, to awaken the minds of all ages of human life that there is a Goal for a Portion of them, and It should never be ignored.

Children must learn that though it is innate in them to want to lead others or accomplish goals, the Greatest Goal that they can reach is within them, to do, to accomplish, by remembering that every act, every action, every thought, every word is important, because through everything they show, they practice, it is recorded in their Soul.

As I leave you now, do not forget, no human being is conceived, in the human way, that is not Gifted with a Soul."

NOVEMBER 26, 2001 AT 12:48 P.M.


## SAINT JUSTIN MARTYR

"**T**his Gift of Divine Love The Father has given to the world of human life at this time, is a Gift beyond anything that a human life could do on his or her own, because so Many Here in the Heavens speak in a manner and way, mainly for the good of millions of Souls.

*The word 'Soul' to a human being, many times, just means Something they are told they possess, but It cannot be seen. Of course, they are also told that the Soul is that Portion of The Creator that is to be returned to Him in Purity, Honor, Dignity, and Love. Human life should find this easy to understand, but many who think about it, hear the Words, use excuses, or I should say find a way to see difficulty in a Statement of this Greatness, this Divine Love.*

There are millions of all ages of human beings throughout the world who see only humanism as the means of life, the way of life, and the only understanding they have of being born a human being.

*The world has been blessed for a very long time, beginning with the history that has been put into script regarding that even The Son of The Creator was an*

*Important Gift of Divine Love, so that all human life would be able to associate with that Portion of The Creator that took upon Itself the form of human life, thus helping human life after that, to more fully understand that if The Creator would put a Portion of Himself in the human form, suffer, and die, for human life to understand that human life has many facets to it, through the minds of all who are born. The very Crucifixion of The Son of The Creator of All Things is evidence that human beings must understand to be a Gift of Divine Love for them, to more fully comprehend that human life can be evil when it should be pure, and act ignorant when they should be kind, understanding.*

I will not speak long on this subject, but it is Important that All that has been delivered through this Gift of Divine Love reach all areas of human life, all languages, all degrees of understanding, that human life was born to one day return a Portion of it to The Creator of All Things.

Ask yourself a very simple question. This should help you better understand how, in a simple way, The Father Instructs The Divine to man. Do you not in some form, some way, allow certain things to occur that will have an impact on others to learn from, and to be able to be stronger in an important area, giving them hope, satisfaction, even love? *You can compare this to the Birth of The Son of The Creator, to the Crucifixion of this Son, and then the knowledge that The Son was returned to Him from Where He had Come.* So be it."

NOVEMBER 27, 2001 AT 12:35 P.M.

**OUR LORD**

"You will be surprised how I Announce Myself to you today. I am The Son Of The Father.

It is Important that all of human life more fully understand that as there are Three In The Holy Trinity, human life is Gifted with a Soul, making human life more than just a human being.

This Gift of Divine Love through which, and in which, so Many Saints have participated with Words Understandable, Words of Direction, Words of Encouraging human life to more fully understand that human life is a Gift of Divine Plan — there are so many Gifts in this Gift: the Gift of ability to see, to touch, to understand, and to have a mentality that can absorb so much learning, so much under-standing in in-depth subjects; also, the ability to be aware that human life's Closeness to The Creator is obvious, because of all the innate blessings that, in many ways, imitate What The Creator is capable of, and in a Loving Way, sharing with human life Gifts that no other living thing possesses.

The world has been blessed at this time, in a way different than other times, but closer to the way the time The Son walked the earth.

As I close My Words with you, I beseech you to always remember, as a human being you are blessed with Divine Love, and this Love can lead you to Heaven. So be it."

NOVEMBER 28, 2001 AT 12:35 P.M.

## SAINT ATHANASIUS

"**I** am Saint Athanasius.  There are Many present Here with Me today.  We All want every living human being to more fully understand what a privilege it is to be born in the way of man.

**M**any of Us Saints beseech The Father to allow Us to act in some form, some way, to discourage an individual from making their Soul impure in any way.  *The Father says: 'Do not forget, I have blessed them with a "Will", and this Blessing is personal to every human child born.  The "Will" is a "Gift of Choice" in what they say, what they do, else they would be not human, and would not be able to understand the importance of purity over impurity, justice over injustice, love over hate.'*

**C**aring is a very important act of love when it encourages, either by one's actions or words, someone else to see the importance of whether an act is right or wrong, pure or impure, just or unjust, kind or unkind, necessary or unnecessary.  The listing on these words is endless, because human life has the *'privilege to choose'*, in all areas of life, what they will partake in, what they will reject, what they will be good example in, and what will have a taint or a total wrong

immorally, in what others see them
participate in, or be example of.

All of the Saints want every human
being born to become a Saint. Think of it this
way: Very often a man, a woman, a child will
take great pride in how they appear to others
physically, or psychologically, domestically or
intellectually. It is important that one word
be added to this: What does one's stature,
words, actions imply as to whether it is
thoughtfulness, good example, or morally
sound or immoral in its own way?

All ages learn from what they see, what
they hear, and there is a great impact on how
they respond. Sometimes they imitate,
sometimes they desire to be the one imitated.
There are so many facets to human life,
because in human life there were so many
Gifts included — the ability to see, to hear, to
speak, to act, to walk, and many other
important things that radiate to others good
example or bad example, truth or untruth.
The list is endless.

*This Gift of Divine Love that bears
the Name of The Beloved Foster Father of
The Son of God, gives to the world at this
time, Messages that should never be
ignored, and All the Saints Here in the
Heavens want to take part in this Gift,
because It is a Gift of Instruction,
encouraging those who will follow What
is put into print, the Importance of
human life and the Goal that awaits it; a*

**Goal Higher than any human goal could ever comprehend.**

As I close My Words with you today, I beseech you to be good example, so that others will learn from you and see the Importance of human life as it was designed to be — what would one day have the privilege to return to The Creator, and be called a Saint."

NOVEMBER 29, 2001 AT 1:06 P.M.

## OUR HEAVENLY MOTHER

"I am your Heavenly Mother. We All smile when there is happiness amongst those who are present.

It is important that all of human life understand that to be a human being is a privilege, because it has a Purpose, it has a Goal, it has a beginning, and basically there is no end to it, because the Soul is the survivor and will live on Forever.

We hear so many individuals mention that they would like to leave a mark for others to remember; some form of a heritage that would keep their name in front of others at a later time. I smile when I say My next Words: 'The best way to allow this to happen, to cause it to occur, would be to practice, in everyday life, your will, your way, your Goal, to become a Saint.'

Sainthood is a reality, as you know reality to be. It exists in an obvious manner and Sainthood is Forever, not for just a period of time, governed by how you feel, how you live, how you work, or on things you enjoy.

My Words today are delivered with much Love, much Sincerity, and much Hope.

It has often been spoken through this Gift of The Father's Love, to strive to make your Goal Sainthood. It is not an impossible task; it is far easier than you think, because you are the custodian of all you do, how you treat others, and do not forget, life without a Goal would be empty in many ways, but knowing that you have a Portion of The Creator within you, should make life worthwhile in every day, because you do have something to look forward to. There is a Purpose for why you were born, and all the understanding you have on human life because you are living it, but also that you automatically have a Goal for a Portion of you called the 'Soul'.

The Soul will live Forever. A lot depends upon your role in the human way, Where the Soul will be placed at another time, another way.

As I leave you, I bless you, because as you use your time to try to better understand, to more fully comprehend the Purpose of human life, you always have that Goal.

As I leave you on this day, I only leave you with My Words. I am Forever near you and ready to hear what you have to say."

DECEMBER 2, 2001 AT 9:00 A.M.

"In the creation of human life, God instilled in this Special Gift of His Divine Love, many things that He had. The Gifts are numerous in number, but rarely, if ever recognized, is the *'Source'* of these Gifts.

No other living matter or thing has the full in-depth ability to think, act, or practice so many innate forms of logic, understanding, abilities that are numerous in number; also, the conscience of what is right to think, act, practice, or be mentally aware of it being pure over impure, just over unjust, right over wrong, logical or illogical.

The knowledge of so many subjects, giving to human life abilities of understanding *in-depth creativities* to aid human life mentally, morally, physically, socially, and above all, understanding that there has to be an ***Ultimate Source of life that created all things***, thus instilling into human life, the ***Goal*** is ***Special and Divine***."

DECEMBER 3, 2001 AT 1:01 P.M.

## SAINT MARGARET MARY ALACOQUE

"**I** am Saint Margaret Mary Alacoque. As The Father has directed me to speak at this time, I thank Him for the privilege to be able to represent The Divine.

There are so many Blessings that human life does not see, feel, or understand. It is sad for All of Us Saints when We see So Much Divine Love every moment of every day, and those who are yet in the state of human life are not aware.

*Today as I speak, it is to encourage more love for The Holy Trinity, more respect for The Divine, and more understanding that there is a Goal to life beyond what the human mind could understand.*

As I speak the Words I am speaking, I want you to understand that it is a privilege for All the Saints Here in the Heavens to be able to communicate with human beings through this Special Gift of The Father's Love for His creation, human life, from Above.

So many men, women and children ignore the beauty of what human life is, and was, created for. They take and use each day in a manner and way that it was not designed for.

Today as I speak through one small voice, I request with Deep Divine Love that All that has been delivered through this Gift The Father has so Generously given, to help all of human life to more fully understand, to better understand, to logically understand, that to walk in the human way is Part of Divine Plan, because each human being is Gifted with a Soul, a Portion of The Creator. If this were not so, human life would not have all the abilities that it has been endowed with, to help all ages understand there has to be a Goal for being created as man.

We see so many men, women and children ignore the Purpose for their lives. They cater to all that is immoral, impure, unclean, because they want only to feel they are satisfying the human being.

*As I close My Words today, I beseech you to look at each day as a step closer to being blessed with The Father's Love for the Soul that is a Portion of Him that you are Gifted with, because this Gift of His Divine Love within you, is to give you the strength, the courage, the ability, the love to return to Him What is rightly His.*

So many of Us Saints are eager to speak through this Gift of Divine Love because, do not forget, it is Our Souls that Speak, not the physical way We lived, but That Portion of the One Who created all things is used in a manner, way, degree, to help millions of Souls be returned to Him from Where They came, to give human life a Special Gift that nothing else has.

　　As I close My Words, I beseech you to read Them in the Full Measure They are meant, because All that has been delivered for some time now, is a Gift of Divine Love that *nothing* can compare to."

DECEMBER 4, 2001 AT 12:51 P.M.

## SAINT CATHERINE OF SIENA

"**I** am Saint Catherine of Siena.  I come today to speak on two very important subjects; one is on the morals of human life.

The Father, in giving to the world the Commandments that He Willed mankind to follow, and to understand as the Guidelines for human life, are being cast aside by millions of men, women and children.

When The Son of The Creator was born, it was for a Very Important Reason, because the Presence from childhood on was to give strength to the birth of a human being, and what the human life was to stand for; a constructive format for living as a human being, one of honor, one of truth, and one that would give to all others a strength to more fully understand that human life had a Goal, and each human being is given the privilege to achieve the Goal for their Soul, because of how they act amongst those who walk the same role, the human role.

*Today as I speak, I must further announce that The Father has given to the whole world of human life a Gift similar to when He gave to twelve men the opportunity to instruct, and to be a model of purity of the mind and the body, for the Soul.*

My Words are Important because in Them The Father's Love shows.

Today is an important day in the life of every human being alive, because today each human being has the opportunity to see the importance of human life, and that through their will they can achieve a High Goal, Higher than any goal in the human life, commonly known as Sainthood for the Soul.

We hear some individuals question what the Soul is. The Soul is a Portion of The Creator, because without this Gift of Divine Love, human life would not have the abilities, the knowledge, or a goal.

*As I close these Words, I beseech you to take the responsibility upon yourselves to spread this Gift of Divine Love that bears the Name of The Beloved Holy Spirit of The Creator, called 'Saint Joseph'. In the human way 'Joseph' was an important name, but then there was a point when the word 'Saint' was automatically added to the name, giving to all of human life the Importance of the creation of human life, and through the Birth of The Holy Spirit, the human birth, it openly addressed the subject that God, in His Love for human life, showed that the human way is Important, so He gave a Portion of Himself to prove His Point.*

As I close My Words, I want you to remember, all who read these Words, it does not take a brilliant mind to understand that human life was created by The Divine, and bears a Portion Unseen but *always present* from the moment of conception.  It's called the *'Soul'*.  So be it."

DECEMBER 5, 2001 AT 12:55 P.M.

## SAINT IRENAEUS

"**I** am Saint Irenaeus.

**T**he Father, in His Great Love, Deep Concern for human life, has given this Gift, helping all ages, all degrees of intellect, all backgrounds of human life, to more fully understand, to more deeply comprehend, the importance of spiritual understanding in the right text, content of its full measure.

**W**e hear so many men, women and children say that they pray, but they do not get an answer. *Many times the Answer is very obvious, but actually given in a Deeper Concept than the individual understood the Value, the Meaning, and the Divine Love that interceded, and gave a Gift Greater than the individual or individuals realized.*

**M**any children pray a short prayer to pass a test that they personally knew that they did not have the knowledge, but the challenge had to be met. Many adults pray for matters, situations, conditions, but they do not provide the amount of personal participation that it takes to accomplish what they will to accomplish; they feel prayer will do it for them.

My Words are different on this conversation, because as My Words are being put into script, I read the minds of those who write the Words, and then those who will read the Words at another time will have to look at the Words and judge the Words in the Reality of the Real Meaning, the Real Perception and, of course, more fully understand the Purpose for the Words to be spoken in a request manner.

I close My Words with you today, because it is important that men, women and children see the value of how they think, what they wish for, and how deeply their commitment can be to *follow what is morally correct, morally pure for the Soul that they are the custodian of.*

As I close My Words, I close Them with a deep love for human life because, do not forget, I, too, took part in this life."

DECEMBER 6, 2001 AT 12:46 P.M.

## SAINT JOHN OF THE CROSS

"**I** am Saint John of The Cross.

**T**hroughout the world there is little understanding of the Importance of believing in a Divine Family.

**S**o many read Bible History, and they try to implant into what they have read, interpretation that allows them to only think of humanism, ignoring the Importance of What is called 'Divine'.

**W**e hold the little one tightly, for there are Many of Us Here, *because a Blessing of this Magnitude is unknown to human man.* The Father has given to the world a Gift of Divine Love, to help all ages of human life to more fully understand that there is a Purpose for all a human being thinks, says, practices, and can fully understand. Without these things, it would be impossible for human beings to innately know there is a Goal beyond the human role.

**T**his Gift of Divine Love that The Father has given to the world, is a Gift beyond what any human mind could relate to in the manner that so much, thus far, has been delivered, could be done on a human being's own understanding of the importance of human life, and its Goal.

There are millions of men, women and children throughout the world who find it easier to deny this Gift of The Father's Love, because they do not want to be controlled. It is not just *foolishness*, nor is it just what man would call *'ridiculous'*. It is beyond both these words. There is only one word to use that fits the situation, and that is the minds of so many so-called learned men and women are **demonically controlled.** They feel that they have the power to understand all things, but basically they accept only what they feel is satisfactory to them, or beneficial to them, but also, that they have a personal control.

I will close My Words, because What I have spoken is of Great Importance, and must be seen for how well The Father knows what is occurring to so many human beings, encouraging them to ignore the Commandments that were given a long time ago, and the importance of each individual caring for their own Soul.

A foolish question arises so many times: 'If I have a Soul, why can I not see It?' The very fact that you know right from wrong, good from evil, tells you that there is more to you than the physical, or your own will to act inappropriately at any time.

*I close My Words through this small voice, but hopefully, that soon All that has been delivered through this Gift of Divine Love will be seen for the Importance It is, because nothing greater*

***could have been given to human life,
helping all ages to understand they are
the possessor of a Portion of Divine Love,
Divine Being, that nothing else is, has, or
will ever have.*** So be it."

DECEMBER 7, 2001 AT 12:58 P.M.

## SAINT CATHERINE OF SIENA

"**I** am Saint Catherine of Siena.

The Father has blessed the world with a Gift Greater than mankind can possibly, fully understand. The Gift is to give to human life of all ages, all degrees of intellect, all talents, the ability to understand, comprehend mentally, *that human life was created for an Ultimate Goal, because of the Soul that human life is the custodian of, from the moment of conception until The Father decrees It to be in the Place It has earned through the one in whom It was placed, presented, given, at a particular time, to walk in the world.*

Children are not being instructed that the Creation of human life has an Ultimate Purpose, a Goal beyond any human goal that can be achieved or desired to be. Many times there is so much value put on materialism. This is not always wrong, but when it supersedes the importance of one's way of life that deals with an individual's moral practices or immoral practices, it is of Great Importance that the individual think more about what human life was created for, and that without a Goal there would be no reason to understand purity over impurity, justice over injustice, right over wrong, good over evil.

As I close My Words, *it is Important that All that has been delivered through this Gift of The Father's Love for human life be seen for what a Great Worth It is, for the human mind, for the body of the human being, but also for the Goal for the Soul that is placed at the moment of an individual's conception.*

When We hear individuals say, 'How do I know I have a Soul?' this statement is an excuse, because an individual can believe in so many different unrealistic values. *Why can they not believe in the logic of being born with a Portion of The Creator, because purity of the mind is innate in a human being, and it is Important that every human being understand that this Gift alone bears witness to the Importance of That Portion of human life, the Soul.* So be it."

DECEMBER 10, 2001 AT 1:08 P.M.

## OUR HEAVENLY MOTHER

"**I** am your Heavenly Mother.

This Gift of The Father's Love for all of mankind is a Gift beyond what any human being can possibly, fully comprehend.  A Gift comparable to this was the time He walked the earth in a human way, teaching and giving to men close to Him the privilege to work with Him, and to fully understand that human life was Gifted with Divine Plan.

If there was no goal to human life, no reason for purity of the mind, would not human life be like animal life, not able to judge or to mentally use an intellect to more fully understand all there is for human life to learn about, to practice, to be a part of, and to know that human life has a Goal?

This statement should be easy for all ages to understand, because it is innate in the human mind to want to do many things, to learn about many things, to understand the value of what they have, what they are, what they do, and also, to understand that they are different than all other things created, because other things do not have the mentality or the reality of all that surrounds them, what it is for, and how it will help them mentally, physically, morally.

An animal does not think of morals. Trees do not think, they grow, and no matter how beautiful they are, they are merely a plant in the ground to aid the lives of human beings in some form, some way, some degree, that gives to human beings what they need, whether it be shade or something in a decorative manner, or there are several other things, bearing fruit.

I could go on endlessly on all the things that are created to help human beings of all ages in how they live, how they think.

Today as I speak, I speak differently, because The Father has given to the world a Gift of Assurance to human life, and also the understanding to realize that human life has a Portion of life within them that will remain when the physical no longer exists. This Life, of course, is called the 'Soul', a Portion of The Creator, because of Divine Love for human life.

As I leave you, always remember, I am only a thought away, and when you pray your prayers are heard, no matter what you say."

DECEMBER 11, 2001 AT 12:47 P.M.

### SAINT IGNATIUS LOYOLA

"**T**here are Several of Us present. It would be difficult to tell people how Many of Us are always present, because Many of Us go in and out, checking where the little one is, and what is occurring.

**I**, Saint Ignatius Loyola, find a great sadness that those men 'who claim' to walk in the Name of The Creator, are not accepting the work that is attached to this profession of life, due to the fact that this profession is oriented to instructing, to helping, to giving strength to the human way, so that the Soul of each one will be able to return to The Father a Saint.

**A**ll of Us present today speak at different times through this Gift of The Father's Love. Many times We do not mention Our Names. Ask yourself, *if there was no real purpose for life other than the one you live each day, would there be any need for the Commandments that were given for the sake of your Souls? Also, what would be the purpose to pray, who would you pray to, why would you pray? I also ask, 'What goal would you have for the physical life that you live, bearing knowledge, understanding, and all the facets of life that cause human life to be special in so many ways?'*

As Many of Us Saints gather, We do it because it is The Father's Will, to remind millions of human beings that there is more to life than what they live each day. So many times We see individuals strive to reach goals that, in so many ways, is just a momentary satisfaction. *Needless to say, the Greatest Goal should be Sainthood, because through this Achievement there are so many Beautiful Gifts that The Father extends to the Soul that reaches this point of success.*

There are so many ways to say the Words I have just spoken, but there are many reasons for them to be spoken, because rarely, if ever, do most men, women and children live one day thinking of what a privilege it is that they have a Goal to reach, designed by The Creator of All Things.

Humanism is common to human life, but logic says human life with all its talents, abilities, gifts, should realize *there has to be a Goal, because The Father, in His Love for human life, only stops the physical, and the Soul is the recipient to go on and on and on, returned to Him a Saint.*

Human beings ignore this fact, this possibility, because they say, 'I cannot see a Saint with the name of anyone I know, or knew.' This, of course, is human theory, human acceptance, but in many ways foolish, because human life was designed with so many gifts, so logically it would have a Goal for That Portion of It, the Soul.

Please remember All these Words, and never forget, The Son of The Creator of All Things was put upon the earth to be Example, to give Strength, so that when the History of His Life would never be erased, it would give hope to all of human life, that the *obvious fact* was available through The Son of The Creator, because He returned to From Where He Came.

As I bless those who print My Words, and who will read My Words, I beseech you, *make each day important, because each day you have, gives you the ability to more fully understand that within you, you have the privilege to make your Soul a Saint.*"

DECEMBER 12, 2001 AT 1:18 P.M.

### SAINT TERESA OF AVILA

"**I** am Saint Teresa of Avila.

There are so many errors being performed regarding what is morally right, wrong, pure, impure, just, unjust. The words are endless.

*In so many ways, the importance and the purpose for which the Commandments were given to human life was to give men, women and children the Rules that would give them Sound Direction in all they did, all they said, and all they willed to be done.* In so many areas of the world, the Commandments of The Father's are eliminated, thus encouraging human beings of all ages to be guided by the rules of human beings, who supposedly stand in authoritative places.

Children are not being instructed on the importance, the joy, and the purpose for why they should be pure in their minds, and not allow anyone to cause them to perform impure acts, thoughts, speech. There is so little sound direction by those in charge of children, basically denying the children the Importance of what The Father Wills them to follow, to practice, *and to understand that they were created to one day return a Portion of them to Him.*

The beauty in the realization of the birth of human beings is lost, has been lost, to basically demonic reasoning. It is difficult for many, of all ages, to fathom that they can be the victims of something they cannot see, cannot hear, cannot feel, so they respond in manners, ways and degrees totally impure, regarding their body, their mind, with no thought, of course, that they are the custodian of a Soul, a Portion of The Creator that He Wills them to return to Him Forever.

There are so many theologians who do not understand the basics of what purity means. They become so involved in theory, or their interpretation of what they read, what they learn, that there is very little sound instruction physically, or through the written word, from them, by them, because of them.

*I could speak hours on this subject, as All of Us Saints Here in the Heavens could. This Miracle of The Father's Love has been given to all of human life with the Written Word, through so Many Saints Here in the Heavens, because All that was previously put into script is not always clearly understood because of its manner of content, and also, the imagination of those, or I should say some of those, who had the final word on what they felt The Father meant.*

Always remember, when you or someone else refers to The Father in Heaven, the word 'Father' does not fulfill the Full

Meaning of The Creator. In many ways, it is an intimate association when the word 'Father' is used; a close association, *but all ages of life must understand that the One called 'God' is The Creator and The Judge, the Justice and the Hope that will one day be what the Soul of all human life will see and understand.*

Theologians may argue this point, but I assure you, All that is delivered through this Gift of Divine Love, is for the Souls that each human being is the custodian of, Who will be able to return to Heaven."

DECEMBER 13, 2001 AT 11:40 A.M.

## GOD THE FATHER

"**I** have blessed the world with an Open Sign of My Divine Love, through one voice, one instrument, one solely doing My Will, for the Salvation of millions of Souls.

Those present with her are gifted with a privilege of My Love. Those who will read the Words, learn from Them, will find strength, hope, and more understanding of My Existence and the Goal I have for all of human life, because *within human life I placed a Portion of Myself.*

This *'fact'* should be obvious, because all other living matter or thing does not have the ability of understanding, or are they gifted with the talents that I have placed within human life; first of all, a mental process of being able to learn, not as an animal learns, but with great in-depth understanding of so many, many things.

As I use one small body, I use a love she has for Me, and it is through this 'association of mutual understanding' that So Much is able to be given to all human beings.

The child questions translation so others will have the Benefits that she sees through the Written Words of ordinary language. I always smile at her love and sincere desire for all nations of human life to be granted what I Will them to know, so they will have the privilege of understanding that within them they bear a Portion of Me, that at a given time will be returned to Me, representing from whom It came and the conditions under which They were treated in My Name.

As I leave you, those who take My Words and hear My Words, I remind you, you have been blessed by this Gift of Sacrifice through one child such as you, who serves Me, so that millions of Souls will have the opportunity to be returned to Me in Purity. So be it."

DECEMBER 13, 2001 AT 12:58 P.M.

## SAINT JOSEPH, THE HOLY SPIRIT

"I am Saint Joseph. This Gift of The Father's Love is Far Greater than any human being can comprehend It to be, because It is a Gift of Instruction, of Direction, Hope, and Much Love.

The small voice that is used to speak the Words He Declares for millions of men, women and children to one day read, must never be cast aside, because All that has been delivered is strength to every human being, and It will be strength for those to come at a later time.

Children are not being instructed on The Divine. Throughout the world there is so much irresponsibility in the importance of human life, and the Goal that it was created to one day reach. So-called 'highly learned' individuals of all backgrounds, many times find more strength, more interest in subjects that have no connection to how they should live, and the Goal they should try to reach at another time.

Humanism is a word meant to express a certain creation of human life, or I should say of a living matter or thing. Animals do not have Souls, the fish do not have Souls, only human life is the custodian of a Soul.

Today is another day in the life of all who live at this time, but so little thought is given on the time when human life will not be in the state it is today.

The world has been Blessed by a Gift Greater than men, women or children can comprehend It to be.

Many years ago, men were chosen to learn from The Son of The Creator, many important issues regarding human life. The ones close to Him are names to be remembered, but all that was to be learned was not only at that time, because every period of time since then has been given in some form, through someone chosen to express more understanding of The Father's Will, Love, Intentions for human beings, because of the Soul they are the custodian of individually.

I could speak hours on this subject, but it would be too much for some to be able to fully understand, because oftentimes the written word does not register in the minds of all who read it. They just skim over the meaning within it. That is why So Much has been

delivered through this Gift of The
Father's Love, all because there are so
many who will gain Hope, Grace, and
much Direction in how much of It they
understand, and the reality of why they
were born in the human way, thus giving
them a Goal to reach one day.

This should not be difficult to
understand, because in so many ways in
the human plan, men, women and even
children strive for success. They know it
is available, and they also know that it
gives them accomplishment for the
physical and the mental, and sometimes
for the monetary. That is why it is so
important that all degrees of human life,
all backgrounds, learn to understand
that human life was not created for just
a period of time, but that a Portion of it
was to be returned to The Father,
because He created human life for a
Reason, a Purpose, a Goal that no other
matter or living thing is the custodian
of.

This Gift of Divine Love, bearing
the Name of The Beloved Saint Joseph,
is openly a Gift of Greatness, of
understanding more about one's life, and
the Purpose for which it was given.

As I leave you, I leave you with
much hope that all who read these Words
will see the Value of Them, the Truth in

**Them, the Hope in Them, and The Divine
Love that shows in telling It in such
Clear Statement, so everyone will
understand more clearly that they were
created as man, for an Ultimate Goal."**

DECEMBER 14, 2001 AT 1:09 P.M.

## OUR HEAVENLY MOTHER

"**I** am your Heavenly Mother.  We All smile, listening to the conversation, bringing to mind the memory of so much that has occurred in this Gift of The Father's Love, for all of mankind.

Today as I speak, it is with Deep Love for all of human life.  It is important that those who follow the Will of The Father bear in mind that all they do, all they think, all they say, and the example they are to everyone else, leaves a mark on their Soul for another time, another way.

Human life was created out of Divine Love, and all the Gifts of human life were to instill in the minds of human beings that they had a Goal to achieve, that nothing else was Gifted with.

So many times an individual thinks about praying, but then forgets about it when they are interrupted by something careless, ridiculous, or just because they are distracted.

Today as I speak, I come through this Gift with more Love than any human being can fully understand.  Human love was designed by The Father.  It was designed after His Love, but of course, not to the Degree of His Love. Love for others, in the human way, has strength in it, purpose, and in many areas gives hope where there is weakness.

So little is talked about what human life is truly all about, and yet men, women and children live it every day. We hear some say, 'I would be praying now, but I am so distracted by all I must accomplish, all I must do, or even say.' Those who think this way should ask themselves, would not it be wise, at a quiet moment, to remember a short gift of thanks, a word of love that no one would hear, and it would be quick to say instead of ignoring the fact that you have this ability, and it doesn't take much time or privacy in the human way?

There is so much to be instructed to men, women and children. That is why this Gift of The Father's Love was given at this time, because there are so many heresies, so much doubt, so much permissiveness, and so many sins of the flesh, of the body, of the mind, causing the Soul much harm.

We hear some say, 'If I have a Soul, why can I not see It, or feel It?' Through your mentality, you know what is pure over what is impure on all subjects; you were given the Gift of being able 'to choose', not just accept.

As I leave on this day, always remember I am not far away, because if there were one million minds thinking of Me, I have the Privilege, the Ability, and The Divine Love to hear what each one will say.

As I close My Time with you now, I beseech you to look at each day as a day closer to becoming a Saint, because the time of the day, what you do, what you say, is always recorded in Divine Way."

DECEMBER 17, 2001 AT 12:52 P.M.

## OUR HEAVENLY MOTHER

"**I am your Heavenly Mother.**

**It is sad for so Many of Us Here in the Heavens to have to see such a small body go through so many preparations, for the sake of human beings of all degrees of intelligence, all backgrounds, and all opinions on what is right, what is wrong, what is true, what is untrue.**

**It is Important that this Gift of The Father's Love for human life be passed throughout the world, even when It is rejected by individuals who cannot believe that they live in a time that so much Love from The Divine is being passed on, and put into script.**

**The world has been blessed, because of the Souls that are being abused by those within whom They were placed at the moment of conception. There is so much diabolical interference that must cease.**

**The Important Statement I am about to make is that the human being who feels distracted by wrong, has the *ability to reject* what is wrong, what is immoral, what is impure, what is unjust. The human mind has the ability to do many things, and weakness is no excuse**

for saying that one is trapped by emotions that they felt would be all right, because of being a human being it is difficult to not do some things.

The little one who speaks Our Words is oftentimes a victim of interpretation, or I should say misinterpretation; also, it can be spoken of as jealousy of those who feel they have the knowledge and the power to make judgment on a Gift of this Magnitude, that basically is Sound in Its Reality, Truthful in What It speaks, and Beneficial for the Purpose It obviously is for the mind and the body and the Soul of all ages of human life.

I could speak hours on this subject, because it is so important for men, women and children to realize, not compromise, that in their decisions they must choose what is pure over what is impure, and not make *excuses* called human weaknesses because they will favor the wrong instead of the right.

I will close My Words, because My Words are very heavy on the little one through whom We All speak. By heavy, I mean her will to do The Father's Will, and accept All that is delivered through her, is a responsibility so in-depth within her, that It causes a physical strength to reach exhaustion that is, and will be and always has been, for others

to understand that to speak the Words
commanded to be spoken according to
The Father's Will, takes more strength
than the human minds of others can feel.
So be it."

DECEMBER 18, 2001 AT 1:17 P.M.

## OUR HEAVENLY FATHER

"I am your Heavenly Father.

I placed this little instrument through a very tedious change.  Though it was, and is very difficult on her, within her, it is for the sake of millions of souls that will one day read about this Miracle of My Love for human life.

At the Sacrifice of The One called My Son, much was accomplished, because at that time there was so much doubt to What a Supreme Power Existed. There was so much diabolical interference through actions, through stubbornness, through egotism, and through the inability to accept the Importance that My Son stood for in the human way.

Jealousy comes easy to human life, and there are so many various degrees, reasons of jealousy, but jealousy, in many ways, destroys valuable relationships, interests, productivity, and yes, love where it is needed.

So many times when this little one speaks, the Words are from One of Us, because she is innately quiet by nature, but also, by her own volition.

The world has been given a Gift Greater than it wants to see It as, because throughout the world there are so many individuals who live totally on the values that they feel are necessary for their lives to be pleasant to them, and valuable in certain areas where they are associated to situations, conditions, or popularity. The word 'popularity' is almost an annoying word to speak, because so many times, so much wrong is attached to popularity. It does not bear within it the beauty of fully understanding the importance of human life, and that human life is Gifted with a Portion of The Creator.

This statement is difficult for many to understand. Some make foolish remarks, insulting to the facts.

Today as I speak, I speak with Deep Love and Concern, because in this Gift of So Much being spoken and put into print, should encourage all who read the Words to know and to understand that no human being would think this way, or feel that a Greater Degree of Life Exists, and it is This Life that has Created All Things, not the one that they live in a personal form, way, degree, with limited abilities on all things.

As I close My Words with you, I
beseech you to fight against all obstacles
with dignity, with assurance, and with
love for others to fully understand that
human life was created to one day return
to The Creator, a Saint."

DECEMBER 19, 2001 AT 12:51 P.M.

SAINT AGNES

"**I** am Saint Agnes. It is a privilege for me to partake in this Gift of The Father's Love for all human beings throughout the world.

**A**ll of the Saints Here in the Heavens cherish these moments that The Father gives to Them, to speak through this Gift of His Divine Love.

**I**t is so Important that men, women and children begin to recognize the value, the privilege, and the Divine Love that is given for each birth of human life.

**T**oday as I speak, I want all who read the Words to know that *the Goal for the Soul of human life is Far More Beautiful, and a Generous Gift from The Father's Love, because the Soul is the Remaining Portion that, in many ways, is the recipient of all an individual was gifted with, and how the individual dealt with all actions, all features of human life.*

**S**o Many Saints Here in the Heavens smile when One of Us speaks. We call It a privilege to be able to give Words of Encouragement, more Understanding to those who are yet in the human way, and have a Soul that is the recipient of all that the individual takes part in, practices, does.

Today, as Many of Us gather — because usually when there is One of Us, there are More — there is so much Hope for this Gift of The Father's Love to travel throughout the world, because It is a Gift that nothing in the world can compare to. It is a Gift of Divine Love for the Souls, but also for the individuals who are the ones that will one day stand before The Creator, for all they have done, all they practiced in the human way. The Soul is the recipient, but the individual man, woman or child *will be aware* of what The Father Chooses for the Soul that they were the custodian of at a given time.

We hear some say, 'Well, I won't be alive, so how will I know?' *Human life has many entities to it, and the Communication of your Soul with The Divine will help you be aware of What Takes Place at a Very Important Time.* So be it."

DECEMBER 26, 2001 AT 12:52 P.M.

### SAINT FRANCIS OF ASSISI

"**I** am Saint Francis of Assisi.  My Words flow through a small voice, but They are possible through the Power of The Living God.

It is sad for me to say, too few men, women and children want to understand the Beauty and the Divine Love that they are the recipients of when they are born in the human way.  There are many privileges to this Gift of Divine Love, not always understood the human way, but show themselves in various ways; first of all, through human mentality, understanding, and the ability to learn many things outside of an individual's way of life.

***The world has been blessed abundantly,*** and it is sad for me to say there is more attention on foolish ideas that have no logic, reason, purpose or goal.  The importance of human life gives all human beings the abilities to fully understand that ***there is a Creator Greater than the human mind can comprehend.***

It is important that little ones be instructed regarding the fact that there is a Goal to life, for life, within life, that nothing else has.

We hear so many so-called learned men and women openly speak in justification of their immoral actions, practices and example that, in many ways, is destructive wherever it is shown. Not only small children are the recipients of this impure way, but many adults accept what they see, they hear, they feel, because they automatically use the human role as justifiable, in even wrong things.

Throughout the world there are many so-called 'religious learned' individuals who, in daily life, accept what others think, practice, even when it is diabolical in nature, and an insult to the Commandments of The Creator. *There is no thought as to what is right over what is wrong, what is pure over what is impure, what would be pleasing to The Creator, The Father, The Giver of life, over what is pleasing to the enemy of all these things.*

Children are not being instructed, and it is sad for me to say, many who have grown into many years do not see the importance of human life. They allow themselves to be vulnerable, using the word 'vulnerable' in a very lax manner of acceptance, thus not wanting to admit that they knew what was right over what was wrong, what was pure over what was impure, what was just over what was unjust, what would be pleasing to The Father over what would be displeasing to Him, and pleasing only to the enemy of all things.

The Purpose of this Gift, at this time, that has been given to the whole world of human life — granted, some not ready to read It or understand It, because of the language in which It is put into script, but translations must begin because it is important for Souls throughout the world to know that The Father's Will has been given to human life, and so much Instruction is Important because of the Souls that every human being, not restricted to one language, is the custodian of.

*The Soul is a Portion of The Creator, God Himself, that must be protected and never used in an impure manner, way, or purpose.*

*This Gift of Divine Love that bears the Name of The Beloved Holy Spirit of The Creator of All Things has, in many ways, shared with All the Saints Here in the Heavens, the importance of human life and that it has a Goal Greater than any goal in the human way.*

As I leave you, I only leave you with My Words. I am never any distance from you. *Remember this."*

DECEMBER 26, 2001 AT 1:30 P.M.

## SAINT TERESA OF AVILA

"**I** am Saint Teresa of Avila.

**T**he Father has given to the world a Blessing beyond what a human mind, nature or abilities could possibly make up, to remind others regarding all there is, in regard to the Purpose for which human life was created.

*Human life is gifted with a Portion of The Creator, called the 'Soul'. The Soul is a 'Living Matter' that is to be returned pure when the physical life of a human being no longer exists.*

**I**t is sad for me to say that life, in the human form, is not understood in the Value it is, the Beauty, or the Purpose for which it was created a long time ago. So many men, women and children abuse this Gift mentally, morally, physically, and of course, spiritually. Knowing that this Gift is 'special', all ages should understand that the very fact that the human mind is able to understand the importance of many things, it should be fully aware of the importance for which the body was created, and the intellect was instilled so that an individual could fully understand more than an animal is capable of.

**T**hroughout the world there is much confusion on what human life is all about, because throughout the world the weaknesses in the human beings has allowed, have allowed, and are yet allowing demonic pleasures to be more interesting than what they know they should be doing, they should be thinking, and that is, *to prepare themselves to one day return to The Father that Portion of Him called the 'Soul'.*

How individuals can understand that Saints do exist and not want to become One, it is illogical, because in many ways, the human mind wants success, wants to be popular, wants to be important. This is innate. I ask you then, 'Why is the *Highest Goal* for human life not thought about more, and not used as the focal point in all one does, to arrive as a *Saint* when the time comes?'

It is so easy to ignore a subject of great importance because it changes one's attitude, aptitude, interest, and draws them from a totally humanistic evaluation of what human life is all about.

I close My Words with a serious thought: All through life, men, women and children seek goals. Would it not be foolish to not seek the *Greatest Goal* available for one's Soul, and that would be *to make It a Saint*? So be it."

DECEMBER 28, 2001 AT 12:30 P.M.


SAINT ANGELA MERICI

"**I** am Saint Angela Merici.

**T**he little one whose voice I use to speak to all of mankind, at one time said to me, 'I don't know anything about you, yet I know you are a Saint, so please help me in what I am about to say.'

**S**he continued on with her requests. We All smiled at the sincerity in how she felt in her communication, even when she could not hear the return of My Words assuring her.

**F**aith is a Beautiful Gift of The Father's Love, because it closes the gap between The Divine and a human mind. There is strength in it, courage in it, trust in it, and an indescribable love in it.

**I**t is sad that millions of men, women and children ignore the closeness they have to The Divine every moment of every day, all the time.

**M**y Words will be short, but I felt the Words should be spoken, because there is so much yet to be accomplished through this Gift of The Father's Love for all of mankind.

**L**anguage can be no barrier, mentality can be no barrier, because through the Faith an individual has in the mind toward The

Divine, permits no barrier to interfere with the communication.

As I close My Words, I fully understand the tears the little instrument sheds, because when you know Truth and you see it unjustly used, it is like a human crying.

The Father, in His Love for human life, has given the world a Gift for all ages, all cultures, and wants them to more fully understand that human existence has a Purpose in Divine Plan."

DECEMBER 28, 2001 AT 1:30 P.M.

## SAINT ATHANASIUS

"**I** am Saint Athanasius. We All smile when the little instrument of The Father's Love feels Our Presence and waits for One of Us to deliver *Words of Direction, of Caring, of Love, from The Divine.*

**C**hildren are not being instructed on the importance of prayer or sound reasoning regarding All that is spiritually helpful, and ready to hear from all human beings of all ages.

**T**he world is saturated with so much demonic ugliness, but it is never equal to the Degree of Divine Love that is available for all of human life.

**I**n so many places, so much is accepted that is not helpful to the mental or the physical welfare of all degrees of human beings, thus making some areas of life vulnerable to weakness that should not be acceptable to any age, any background of life.

**S**o many Saints Here in the Heavens would talk constantly through this Gift of The Father's Love because of the Importance of the Souls of all human beings, no matter where they are from, or to what degree of knowledge they are gifted with. Knowledge, in many areas, has a Blessing to it when it is handled in the proper way, but Faith in The Creator of All Things is more logical than many men, women and children understand it to be.

You do live in a time worse than many other times in the history of human life. That is why it is so important that All that has been delivered through this Gift of Divine Love, be spread into lands throughout the world, even when it is suspected or known that there is a language barrier that does not reveal itself in the full meaning It was spoken at a given time.

Feature it like this: *Even if an individual held a Crucifix with no understanding as to what It was all about, the individual would feel 'something', because The Father, in His Love for human life, would give His Touch of Divine Love to the Object and to the individual, helping them to know that What they were holding had a Purpose, a Reason, and had to be formed for a particular Goal.*

So many men, women and children try to ignore All that is given to help them more fully understand that *human life has a Goal, not always called 'Heaven', but there is a Goal to be returned to The Father because of an individual's Soul,*

*that is a Portion of The Creator, that He*
*will return to Himself through a means*
*and a manner that He first gave It,*
*unknown by mankind, but definitely*
*through Divine Will and Way."*

JANUARY 2, 2002 AT 12:52 P.M.

## SAINT JOSEPH, THE HOLY SPIRIT

"**I** am Saint Joseph.

I come to speak on this day, because through The Father's Love for human life, He has given this day to allow thousands, hopefully millions of men, women and children to more fully understand the privilege it is to be born as man.

So much in Bible History allowed the revealing of how each generation learned, regarding the importance of human life, and that *the importance of human life was so important to The Father that He gave a Portion of Himself to the world as a 'man'.* This Step of Divine Love was, and is, far more Important and Greater than human beings of all degrees of intelligence can fully comprehend or understand.

Human life has a Goal, a Goal Greater than any human goal that is addressed in different areas of life, such as occupation, greater education, or monetary measures. The Goal for the Soul of human life is to return to The Father, bearing the name of the one in whom It was placed at a given time.

The birth of a child is important, not just to those who are called the parents, but important to the whole world, because every human being born has the ability to lead others in many ways, because of the Soul that every human being is Gifted with at the moment of conception.

It is innate in human life to want to be successful in so many areas, on so many subjects, sometimes just to be important in the eyes of others, but the Greatest Goal that human life can reach for, is not for their intellect to be outstanding, not for their popularity to be prominent, but for the Soul that is a Portion of The Creator to be returned to The Creator a Saint, representing the one in whom It was placed at the moment of his or her conception.

It is only logical, with all the attributes of human life, that human life would have a Goal different than any living matter or thing, and the beauty of this is that The Father has allowed human beings of all backgrounds to realize and to innately know, that at the end of human life and all its abilities, there had to be, has to be a reason for this individual to have been born a human being.

It is time that all of mankind awaken to the fact, the realization and the logic, that no human being is not gifted with success for the life they lead, thus the success meaning a Goal Higher than human life was, as they lived it.

I know I speak strongly, but I speak with a Love, to The Creator first, because there is no Gift Greater than Divine Love in every aspect of Its Way, Its Will, for things to be exceptional and important.

I bless you with The Father's Love, and I also say: Return the love, because in returning the love to Him you are returning the Soul in the purity He once gave It a long time ago."

JANUARY 4, 2002 AT 12:43 P.M.

## SAINT ALPHONSUS LIGUORI

"**I** am Saint Alphonsus Liguori.

It is sad for Many of Us Here in the Heavens to have to alert those who are yet upon the earth in a live state, to realize that they live in a time far greater than Sodom and Gomorrah. As Sodom and Gomorrah was described through Bibles, through speech and through other means, it was not seen as to how detrimental it was to the Souls of millions of human beings, let alone much serious damage occurred in the bodies.

Though it is hard to accept that men and women of all degrees of intellect could accept a time such as Sodom and Gomorrah was so openly practiced, you, at this time, live in a time worse than Sodom and Gomorrah. The only difference is, that for so long there has been so much stress on the importance of belief in God, belief in purity of the mind and the body for the sake of the Soul, but now, as I speak, you would be devastated to see so much diabolical practice amongst human beings.

The Father has given to the world a Gift of Instruction through one voice. Had He chosen many voices, it would have been more difficult for the Lessons to be learned, *but in this Great Blessing so much has been*

***Instructed, and so much has been spoken on the Importance of the Goal for which human life was created.***

**A**t this time in which you live there is so little reference, let alone very, very little dedication to what is morally sound physically and, of course, morally, mentally, and the words are endless to describe this particular facet of understanding how much evil is being acceptable to all ages.

**I** speak with a hurt within me, because through human life all human beings have the ability to choose. They call it a 'free will' to make decisions.

**I** could speak hours on this subject, but there is a sadness in me, even though I am Where I am, because for All Here in the Heavens to see the desecration of so many Souls, in so many ways, become victims of the ones in whom They are placed at the moment of conception.

**I** close My Words at this time, but before I close Them, I hope you will remember that if any kind of impure temptation passes your way, remember, ***a prayer to The Divine will give you the strength to resist, to reject, to decline any act that is impure to your body and mind.***"

JANUARY 7, 2002 AT 12:48 P.M.

### SAINT ALPHONSUS LIGUORI

"**I** am Saint Alphonsus Liguori.

There are so many subjects that human life is capable of learning indepthly on, but there is one subject that many times is avoided, and that is the importance of human life, and that it has a Goal different than any other goal human life chooses.

*I hold the little one tightly, because so Many of Us speak so often, and the Strength and the Power that We use within her is Greater and Different than any human being can possibly understand, or perceive It to be.*

This Gift of The Father's Love was given through one voice. Logic must tell all who read these Words that one voice was sufficient, otherwise there would be, and would have been, confusion regarding the Importance of the Facts that are delivered for the Importance of the Souls of millions of human beings living now, and those who will come at a later date in time.

In other places, and even where you live, there are many human beings who use many means to discredit a Gift of this Magnitude. Of course, each one has a different reason, purpose, justifying discrediting All that The Father Wills human beings to learn about, and to be able to use as Guidelines for their behavior in all areas of human life.

There are many so-called preachers who use this title for attention, but they do not speak What The Father Wills them to speak, because in their interpretations of certain subjects they, most times, use their own interpretation, not allowing the facts to be seen as they were to be understood, regarding the importance of human life, and The Father's Will for the Soul that each human being is the custodian of.

My voice is harsh through this little one, My Words of Great Importance.

It is sad to see all degrees of intellect absorb so much improper, indecent subject matter. Today the world is saturated with a lack of understanding on the *Most Important Part of human life, and that is the Soul that each human being is Gifted with.*

You live in a time worse than Sodom and Gomorrah. You live in a time of rejection, of substitution, and yes, resistance to a better understanding regarding the importance of human life, and that within it The Creator of All Things instilled a Portion of Divine Love that nothing else has.

*This small voice that is used, is a voice that speaks in Honor and Dignity and Love for The Holy Trinity. The Father's Will must be understood, and so*

*much humanistic theory cast to the
deepest portion of the earth, because as it
lays open for the use and obvious abuse it
causes, many Souls will suffer from it,
because of it.*

    As I close My Words, I do it only at this
time because the Power I use is difficult on
this instrument of mine."

JANUARY 8, 2002 AT 12:40 P.M.

### SAINT DOMINIC

"**I** am Saint Dominic.

**A** child stands in fear of reprimand or physical harm. This statement is also true about those who have grown in years. Fear is innate in human life, whether some individuals admit to it or not, because sometimes fear is so ingrained that it does not show until specific things occur to make an individual, or more than one individual, respond.

**W**hen there is any instruction, or it can be called 'teaching' on the importance of and the value of purity in one's way of life, many times it is ignored, because the word purity says to some: I feel like there is nothing I can do because of others observing it, making it out to be indecent, impure, unjust, cruel, and identify only things that, perhaps are normal by nature or in the human race.

**A**s I speak today, I speak with deep love for human life of all ages. It is important that more time is spent on the instruction of prayer, its purpose, *and that prayer is the communication with The Divine that always gives strength, hope, and more understanding because of the communication that has been spoken about, instructed upon, that every* *individual is born with a Soul, with a Guardian Angel. Logically, what more can be said, how close human life is to The Divine?*

At this time throughout the world there is so much diabolical acceptance, preference, and practice. I ask you, those who read My Words: What happened to the sound understanding, realization, practicality that The Creator of All Things still exists, and is present at all times? We see so many men, women and children violate, through their actions, That Portion of The Creator that is within them from the moment of their conception. But it is even more than this; it is a defiance against truth, logic, hope, practicality, and also, belief that The Father would not create human beings to His Image and Likeness without instilling in them a Gift to give them the strength, to give them hope that they are protected constantly.

So few men, women and children take this into consideration. To most it is a casual remark that there is either hell or Heaven, and many times they even brag about their innate feeling that they probably will go to hell for how they think, how they talk, how they act, how they respond to what others believe in.

I know My Words today are unlike Most of What I reveal, but sometimes it is important to alert people of all ages to be aware of what they can become victims of, because of their own lack of seeing things in the reality they are; also, their indifference to what is morally sound, morally good, morally practical.

*I could speak hours on this subject, because The Father has given to the world what Many of Us Saints call Divine Love, not in a capsule form, but in a Form of Communication that can be read and understood for the Value It is, because of the Close Communication, Association that human life was created with, due to the Soul that, as a Portion of The Creator, is also a Portion of human life.*

So many Words have been spoken, instructing in so many ways, for all degrees of intellect to more fully understand that *there is a Goal for human life, there is a Reason for human life, there is a Love for human life, All Divinely Designed for The Ultimate Goal, Sainthood."*

JANUARY 9, 2002 AT 12:47 P.M.

## OUR HEAVENLY MOTHER

"**I** am your Heavenly Mother.

Throughout the world there is much laxness in prayer, in dedication to what is morally sound, correct, pure. There are many men, women and children who are in desperate need of this Gift of The Father's Love, because this Gift is for all intentions, understanding, ideas, values, thoughts, and definitely for how an individual converses with others, and the importance of the subjects that they choose to speak on.

There is so little attention paid to what is morally sound. Conversations ramble on, uttering obscenities, referring it to knowledgeable on the updating of human life. It is important that all men, women and children understand that human life is gifted with what is correct, what is moral, what is right for the mind to partake in, because everything an individual speaks, practices, partakes in, is automatically recorded in the Soul.

This Gift The Father has given to the world, bearing the Name of The Beloved Saint Joseph, is a Gift of Purity, and the Purpose for this Gift is to awaken the minds of all human beings that there is a Goal to life, not physical, not mental, but Higher than these things, and that is to return the Soul to The Father, Pure in All Ways, because The Soul, as a Portion of The Creator, must be Pure before It can enter through what mankind calls *'The Gates of Heaven'*.

As I speak, there are thousands, if not millions of all ages of human life, in sinful actions at this time, ignoring what is morally sound, pure, just, right, never thinking of the Soul that they are Gifted with, that will one day be judged, because the Soul is the Remaining Portion of human life that The Father wants to be returned to Him a Saint.

Becoming a Saint is not impossible; it is extremely possible, because through the Commandments given a long time ago, The Father laid the Outline for how human beings of all ages should control themselves, and feel, see, understand, that the Rules were given because of the innate Love The Creator had for man.

Needless to say, hours could be spent on this subject, but What I have just spoken is to be passed to an unlimited amount of individuals, who need to think about this to help them better understand that they have a Goal

**to reach; it's called *'success as man'*, but then through this *'success'*, The Father once again is the Custodian of the Soul, which is His Plan.  So be it."**

JANUARY 10, 2002 AT 12:32 P.M.

### SAINT ATHANASIUS

"**I** am Saint Athanasius.

Too few people throughout the world care to think about the importance of how they live daily life. So much is taken for granted, and so much accepted that, in many ways, is not beneficial to one's morality, one's spirituality, one's understanding that The Father sees all, because of the Souls that are involved in every human life.

It is sad for me to say, that to most people the Soul is not accepted because It is an indefinable word that is difficult for people of all ages, all backgrounds, to value, *even knowing that It is a Portion of The Creator of All Things.*

Sometimes We hear an individual say, 'I have a pain in my side.' They immediately connect the pain to that portion of the body that they know, or feel, or accept as being in that spot.

Now I take you to your mind. The mentality of human life is beyond what a human being understands it to be. It has multiple Gifts, because The Father instilled into human life what is called a mentality. The mentality is capable of understanding, through the process of hearing, reading, and other ways of learning things that nothing else created has the ability to do; also, the memory is a Gift of Divine Love, beyond what a human being of any degree of knowledge can fully understand.

Children are not being instructed on what a powerful Gift their memory is to them, for them, and it is through the memory, through the mind, that decisions are arrived at according to the mentality, the memory of a human being.

Now let me mention the word 'temptation'. Logic says that temptation, most times, is not for the benefit of one's practice in life, or for the Soul of the individual. It is important that human beings of all ages, all degrees of learning, all degrees of experience with others like themselves, learn to discern what is practical, beneficial, logical, *because every human life is responsible to The Creator at a given time, for all they were involved in physically, mentally, emotionally, spiritually, in their lifetime.*

So Many of Us Here in the Heavens are anxious to speak through this Gift of The Father's Love that delivers so much Personal Concern for the Souls, and for the physical of all human life.

Children must learn responsibility in so many areas, because responsibility gives them strength when temptation enters their way of life.

I close My Words with a Blessing, and I say it in a way that, so many times, has attracted more attention than the words you use every day: ***In Nomine Patris, et Filii, et Spiritus Sancti. Amen.***"

JANUARY 11, 2002 AT 11:52 A.M.

### GOD THE FATHER

"Thousands more of men, women and children must hear of this Gift of My Divine Love that I have given to all of mankind. No race or degree of intellect must not hear of My Love and My Will for human life, because in My Creation of human life, I prepared a Goal of Beauty, Greatness and Divine Love.

I use a little one to pass My Words on to millions of human beings. It is important that All that I Will for them to know — many Saints Here with Me are participating in this — so Souls will be returned to Me that otherwise would be lost to the enemy of all that is Pure, Just, and Important for being returned to Me."

JANUARY 11, 2002 AT 12:40 P.M.

PADRE PIO

"**I** am Padre Pio.

I speak many times through this Great Gift of The Father's Love for human life. I speak in a general form, not mentioning my name, because there would be much controversy in some minds if I were to say, 'I am a Saint, and I speak through a Gift that delivers to all of human life, Divine Love.'

It is important that this Gift be passed throughout the world, for millions of men, women and children to better understand, to more fully comprehend what a treasure it is to be born as man.

The world is in great chaos, not just because of doubts, but because of immorality, impurity of the mind, the body, thus devastating to the Souls of those who commit so many impure actions, thoughts, deeds. There is no purpose to these things, only most times, attention, physical attention. This is sad for me to say, but it is truth, it is fact.

I will close My Words, but I know when it is The Father's Will, I will speak again. So be it."

JANUARY 12, 2002 AT 10:25 A.M.


### GOD THE FATHER

"**T**oo little is being done to accomplish All I Will mankind to be aware of.

It is important that My Words be spread throughout the world. Do not worry about languages. Interpretation of the Words must reach all areas of the world. You will find that the language you speak is more widespread than you know.

I have given this Blessing for **ALL OF MANKIND**, and it is *Important That The Fact That I Am Speaking Is Greater* to the minds of human beings, than sometimes the Words do not compare to.

I send My Love to those who adopt My Will to serve Me, for the sake of millions of Souls yet to be helped by those in whom They were placed at the moment of his or her conception."

JANUARY 14, 2002 AT 12:43 P.M.

## OUR HEAVENLY FATHER

"It will be difficult for many who read these Words to believe that these Words are Mine, that I would speak at a time such as this is, through one small voice, one small body, but one totally dedicated to The Divine.

I am your Heavenly Father. I have given to the world a Blessing Greater than the human mind can comprehend. It is Important, All that has been delivered through this Gift — Some Mine — and Many from the Saints Who are Here with Me.

Though this Great Miracle of My Divine Love is difficult for some to understand or to believe or to accept, is a sadness, but nonetheless, it is only their protection for themselves that they feel it could not be, it could not happen that I, The Creator, would speak through one human voice.

In the creation of human life I had a Great Purpose, and in this Love for this Creation I place a Soul, a Portion of Me, so that each human being will automatically know I Exist, and all things they think, practice or partake in,

My Connecting Link to them— the Soul—
tells Me.

My Words will be difficult for some,
because they cannot comprehend a
Divine Being, but nonetheless, this Gift
of My Divine Love, Instructing in so
many ways, so many times, so much of
My Love, must be seen for the Closeness
I Am to every living human being.

As I speak it is to let you know I
created human life for a Goal that is
above any other goal that human life
could reach.  I beseech you, I plead with
you, *'Return your Soul to Me'.*"

JANUARY 15, 2002 AT 12:33 P.M.

## SAINT IGNATIUS LOYOLA

"**I** am Saint Ignatius Loyola. I have spoken many times through this Gift of The Father's Love for mankind.

There are so many areas The Father Wills for men, women and children to more fully understand what a privilege it is to be born as man. We hear some highly knowledgeable individuals say, 'We have enough right now available to us, what more is there to say?' The Father says to these questions, 'How much do you know about Me, for I created thee in My Way.'

The world is void of many things, even though each human being born has the ability to learn, to understand, and to fulfill many great dreams of accomplishment, of duty, of necessity and, yes, of growth for human life's ability to more fully understand that the Universe is controlled by only One Source of Light, Love, Communication and Ability, thus it is beyond what the human mind can imagine it to be. It is far greater in Depth, in Purpose, in Abilities.

Children are not being instructed properly. They are not being taught about *the Importance of The Creator of All Things.* Everything is imaginary, humanistic, materialistic. These words are endless, that describe the lack of instruction that is being spoken about openly.

We hear some say, 'Only great scientists know so many things, and are able to speak in great detail on them.' Sometimes the most simple phrase can be of the utmost importance to the minds of those listening, such as: *There is a Creator of All Things, and This Creator is The Judge of All Things.*

Human life has the ability to learn many things of great degrees of understanding, but throughout the world most emphasis is put on what mankind calls the *'practical knowledge'* of what they are surrounded by, thus ignoring the Focal Point, The Creator, their words making it appear as though everything just happened, and it's right.

It is so easy for the human mind to want only to accept what they are accustomed to, sometimes in fear that if they learn a deeper degree of what is occurring, it will be frightening to them, too much to handle.

*This Gift of so much Information regarding human life and The Divine, was given for a very Important Reason, because no human mind has the ability to disclose all the Important Facts of The Divine; so The Father, in His Love for this creation of His, has given to the world a voice, not just the written Words, but a voice to speak the Words, making*

*Them more readily understandable to the human mind.*

As I close My Words with you, it is so important that more emphasis be put in everyone's life on *the True Existence of a Divine Power*, and the Importance behind this Power is for the Souls of every living human being, because the Soul is the recipient of all that is accomplished or even practiced, or even thought about. The Soul is not seen, but there is an innate understanding in human life that human life is more than a mere physical thing.

As I leave you, and Many Others Here with Me, We want only the best from your life. The Father Wills it so, and one day you will more fully understand that to be born a human being, to be called '*man*', was a Gift beyond what you understand this Gift to be, *because this is the Only Gift of Divine Love that has a Portion of The Creator within it.*

The word is simple to use when you think it would be nice to once in awhile say, '*I love the Soul God gave me one day, and God, I want to return It to You in the way I understand You Will it to be, and that is for It to be called a Saint*'."

JANUARY 16, 2002 AT 12:53 P.M.

### SAINT CATHERINE OF SIENA

"**I** am Saint Catherine of Siena.

The Father, in His Love for human life, has given to human life the privilege to hear so many Saints speak and be able to read Their Words, so they will remember the Content of the Subject, regarding the Importance for which It was given.

It is difficult for all mentalities of human life to accept, to believe that there is a Goal for human life Greater than the human way. So many times those who preach on this subject do not fully understand, or do they comprehend or do they basically believe what they are saying is fact, is valuable to the mentalities of all who will hear the words.

You do live in a time worse than Sodom and Gomorrah. *'These words'* have been spoken a long time ago, and in many ways. When certain individuals read *'these words'*, they immediately, automatically think, say or wonder why The Father allows human life to be continually born; why The Father does not stop human life from being continued to exist.

In each era of time, human life made decisions, and still make decisions on what they feel is important. They also consider it growth mentally, physically, but how many consider it growth in a spiritual degree that is so astounding that it gives them, or urges them, to more fully understand what a Precious Gift human life is to man? There are always so many discussions on what is occurring, but rarely is there a solution to what is wrong, because too many men, women and children take each day as it comes along.

I feel badly saying my next Words, but it is fact. Sometimes cowardice stops individuals from standing firm on what is morally sound, pure, just, important, and necessary for the Soul, like We hear some say, 'No matter what I would criticize, I will only be criticized in return, so I will not bother with my opinion.'

All of the Saints Here in the Heavens have heard these excuses thousands of times, thus avoiding any conflict, any difference of opinion, ignoring totally that what is morally sound should be an important subject. *What is wrong against sound morals should be spoken out as a neglect to what human life was created for.*

I know what some will think when they read these Words, or I should say, *if* they read these Words. The very same people who would resist speaking firmly on this subject most, would not be concerned about arguing openly on a point that was monetary to them, or how they felt about how they live.

Books could be written on this subject, but I assure you they would not sell, because men, women and children do not see the

Value, the Importance, the Necessity of the Soul they are the custodian of. We hear some say, 'I cannot see It, how do I know It is there?' The very fact that you know justice from injustice, hope from despair, dislike or hate from what is normally called love, you must awaken to the fact that when you do not consider yourself —in a crude manner — *stupid*, then you must have some insight into what is important to human life, and that human life was created for a Higher Goal.

The very fact that human beings of all ages strive for success, strive for attention, strive to be first on issues in places, should prove that human life has the ability to understand that *it is Important to search for the Goal when life ends, to reach for the Goal that awaits each Soul of every human being born — that is to return to The Creator, and be called a Saint.*"

JANUARY 17, 2002 AT 12:40 P.M.

### SAINT ALPHONSUS LIGUORI

"**I** am Saint Alphonsus Liguori.

**S**o many times men, women and children make excuses for what they do, and they call it a 'sign of the times'. Now, if an individual has to make an excuse, I ask you, is it an excuse for doing something unclean, impure, unjust, or is it just an act of politeness on an incident, accident, or a situation that occurred?

**P**rayer is oftentimes said diligently out of habit, but when an individual misses a time, they automatically make excuses to themselves first, and ignore the fact that the prayer was a very important part of communication that gave them strength to accomplish other things, *and also a communication with Someone Who is in a Different Realm of Life, Close to The Father, and able to help, assist without being seen, in answer to prayers of request.*

**I**t is so easy to forget the Goal of life. It is so easy to not remember that a 'thank you' for a favor is heard by the Saint in whom the favor occurred. Though it is difficult for millions of human boings of all ages to truly fathom the Existence of Saints, there are Thousands of Saints available all the time.

**I**f human life had no Goal, it would be a
sadness unbelievable to the human mind,
because the very fact that human life has
been instructed that they have a Portion of
The Creator within them called the Soul,
automatically gives strength to daily living,
and hope in a need at any time in life, just
knowing you are not alone.

**W**hen one in the family passes away,
there is a big void for some time. There is an
adjustment period, but the person is never
fully forgotten because the individual was a
part of the life, in some form, some way, some
degree, and is most times remembered for
little things.

**I**n this Gift that so much is spoken
regarding how Close The Creator is to human
life, it is sad when We see or hear some
individuals ignore the fact that The Father
allows so Many of Us to speak; 'Connecting
Link,' they call It, 'to The Divine,' many
times more natural to believe than an
individual understanding that *The Father is
The Creator of All Things, The Father is
The Controller of All Things, and The
Father is Above and Beyond the human
mind.*

**H**uman life is gifted with hope, and
gifted with the ability to understand what is
pure over what is impure, what is just over
what is unjust, what is kind over what is evil.
Some who read All that is written through
this Gift of Divine Love, openly speak in a

surprised tone, 'It is amazing, the length of Each One Who speaks, in What They say; They are so closely connected in the number of Words.'

Today as I close My Words with you, I remind you, those who put Them in script, and those who will read Them, always remember human life is Gifted with a Soul. It is a Portion of The Creator, not understandable to the human mind, but remember this: How many people have you known throughout your life, and then you do not see them for a long time, but when you meet them, perhaps by chance, it brings back many memories of your association with them.

*I smile when I say these Words, because human life is Gifted with so much Love, due to the fact that human life has a Soul that will one day be returned to The Creator, and as the Soul meets The Creator, there will be a happiness unbelievable to the human mind."*

JANUARY 18, 2002 AT 1:06 P.M.

SAINT PATRICK

"**I** am Saint Patrick.

**S**o many Saints speak through this little voice, giving to others Direction, Love, Hope, so that each one's Soul will be protected, taken care of, and one day return to The Father with the title 'Saint'.

*The Father has given to the world a Blessing beyond what the human mind can fully comprehend or discern. Some like to think What pours through her in Words comes from her, but this is not so. All that has been delivered is The Father's Will for millions of Souls to one day return to The Father Pure, and have the privilege to be called a 'Saint'.*

**T**hink about this: If all human beings born to the world did not have names, wouldn't it be confusing in a hundred ways, perhaps a thousand ways? There would be no way to be able to speak about an individual, and know that the individual truly existed, because the name of a human being is important; it designates an individual, and through this, that individual is responsible for everything he or she does, or even what they speak on different subjects.

**A** person's name, no matter what age they are, has an importance in it; the very fact that when you pray, you are able to designate Who you want to pray to, because of the Name that follows Them all the way to Sainthood. Even The Son of The Creator had a Name.

*Logic must tell you that when you say the Word 'God', you think of only One Individual Who represents That Name. Even when you hear the words spoken, 'God is All Things, God is Everywhere,' it still signifies One Name, One Individual Entity of Living Matter.*

**As** I close My Words with you, I beseech you to always remember that your name is important to more individual men, women and children than you realize. You are remembered because of your name, so remember this: Let nothing cause your name not to be respected, cared about, or not remembered with love, understanding, and as example, when you no longer exist in the human way because, do not forget, *through your name, your Soul has a Distinction that remains with the Soul for All Eternity."*

JANUARY 22, 2002 AT 12:50 P.M.


                              SAINT PEREGRINE

**"I** am Saint Peregrine.

It is important for all of mankind to realize and to understand that *there are Souls Here in the Heavens that came from all walks of life, because the ones in whom They were placed had many personalities, natures, talents, opinions, and challenges that they desired to fulfill in the way of man.*

Children and adults are not looking to what is realistic, what is rational, logical, because though everyone fears death in the human way, they ignore the purpose of death, and that it has a Goal Higher than the individual understands a goal to be.

The Commandments were given a long time ago, through a man, dictated by The Father of All Things.  The Commandments are most times ignored by those who hear Them, or even those who learn indepthly about Them.  We hear so many individuals make claim to understanding the Commandments, but basically do not remember Them when a decision arises, wherein the Commandment should be recognized as the way to handle the situation.

Let us take one Commandment: **'Thou Shalt Not Commit Adultery'**. This Commandment is broken thousands of times a day throughout the world. It is always justified for some human weakness, reasoning, purpose, but innately an individual knows that when they partake in something of this way, it says that their logic is out of control.

So much throughout the world that is wrong is accepted, justifying a weak point in it that satisfies the individual's mind and body, totally ignoring the Soul.

*The Father has given to the world a Gift of Instruction, of In-depth Teaching on the Importance of human life, why He created it, and that it bears a Portion of Him called the 'Soul'.* The very fact that He has announced, through time, that the Soul is a Portion of Him, should not just awaken the minds of human beings to what a privilege this is for them, but a responsibility for how they act; and what about their conscience when they wrongly act, impurely act.

Needless to say, every time Words are spoken from Where I am, They are to instruct men, women and children on the Importance of human life and how The Father Wills it to be, because within it there is a Portion of The Father, unseen, but the very fact that the mentality of a human being has the ability to know what a pure action is over an impure

action, what a just act is over an unjust act.
This list is endless. The words to describe
this list would fill pages of written words.

*A Gift of this Magnitude, giving
insight to all that a human being is
capable of understanding, is truly a Gift
of Divine Love.*

There are no logical excuses from any
human being to deny the importance of what
is moral over immoral, pure over impure, just
over what is unjust. The list is endless.

As I close My Words with you, needless
to say, thousands of pages could be written on
the Importance of human life, why it was
created, and the Beauty of the Goal that
awaits it.

Today as I speak, I speak with a sadness
within me and yet much hope, *because
through this Gift of The Father's Love
that bears the Name of His Holy Spirit,
millions of Souls will one day understand
that the Gift of human life as 'man' was
a 'privilege', and had the Highest Goal of
any living matter or thing.*

Hopefully, My Words will travel far,
because sometimes one individual reading an
Important Message has the ability to spread
the Will of God in many directions, especially
when they feel so indebted to respond to
helping others more fully understand *that
human life is a Gift of Divine Love
Firsthand."*

JANUARY 24, 2002 AT 3:50 P.M.

"**T**he word *'danger'* causes human beings to be alert and concerned because *danger* can mean great harm to the body of those present.

**T**oday, as I speak, I am forced to say, many Souls are in *great danger* of having to suffer because of the ones in whom They are an Important Part of, that Part of The Creator that is given to human life at the moment of conception.

**Y**ou live in a time of many sadnesses to The Father, because there is so much diabolical practicing being accepted by all ages of human life. The Commandments are not being followed correctly; in fact, They are being dismissed as past history of certain generations of life.

**T**his is important to understand, that human life was and is being created for a Goal Higher than any human being can perceive a goal to be — *'**Sainthood for the Soul**'*. Though it is difficult for many so-called spiritual understanding individuals to truly accept as truth and responsibility, it is important that more be put into print on the ***Importance of the Soul*** of each living human being created.

**T**he world is, in many ways, treading on evil analysis, just to give themselves more interesting *'so-called facts'* of the mind. ***This***

*is ridiculous and dangerous*, and it *must cease!* Sins are not to be accepted as normal thinking or characteristic of human behavior. *It is dangerous to the Soul.*

We hear so many ask, 'What is a Soul? I have never seen One.' Yes, you have, and I will discuss this at a later time. But, for now, as your Soul is a Portion of Divine Love, It exists within each human life as the basic understanding of the logic, mentality, and desire in human life that there is a Goal to human life for a Portion of human life. If this were not so, what would human life have to look forward to?

It is innate in the human mind to want to reach goals. Make *Sainthood* yours by being aware of the importance of all you do, say, think, practice, and use for the purity of your Soul, *because The Father wants your Soul returned to Him as He gave It to you — a Saint."*

JANUARY 28, 2002 AT 12:37 P.M.

### SAINT ATHANASIUS

"**I** am Saint Athanasius.

There are many heresies throughout the world, more than an individual human being could fathom it to be. Very few individuals understand what a heresy is. *A heresy is opposite of what is good, what is right, what is moral, what is just, and in many ways, what gives to facts strength, value.*

Today as I speak, I speak differently because there are too many people throughout the world of all degrees of intellect, all backgrounds, who are ignoring how they act, what they practice. They do not look at these human abilities as having the ability to stand for what is correct, feasible, honest, just, or even pure in concept.

I will not speak long, because I find that fewer Words, sometimes, are much more acceptable, understandable, and used for the Value They are when such Words are needed to make a point of a subject more outstanding and more valuable in content.

I have asked The Father if I could bless you, those who take My Words. He smiled and said, *'As you bless those who take the*

*Words, I promise them My Blessing goes with All the Words that flow through this Miracle of My Divine Love for all of human life throughout the world'."*

JANUARY 29, 2002 AT 12:52 P.M.

### SAINT ROBERT BELLARMINE

"**I** am Saint Robert Bellarmine.

In the early time of this Gift of The Father's Love for human beings of all ages, all backgrounds, so Many Here in the Heavens were requested to speak on the importance of human life, and that it had a Purpose and a Goal.

Many times We heard individuals ask what the purpose could be that was so important; if it was so important, then why did not human beings live a longer time? We would all smile at this statement. *Time in life the human way is a privilege, has a Purpose and a Goal. The Goal is not for the body, but for the Soul.*

We hear so many individuals strive to be successful, to benefit others that they know. Remember this statement regarding your Soul, because your Soul has the Greatest Goal above and beyond what the human knowledge, understanding, can perceive a goal as Great as This is, for all human beings.

*So Many of Us have spoken, instructing and enlightening individuals, through Our Words, on the Importance of human behavior, and the necessity for it to understand that through human behavior the Soul is the recipient of all that is spoken, practiced, accomplished, and any part of, in the human way.*

It is so important for children of all ages to be instructed that their physical life has an important role, a Goal available to reach for a Portion of them that no one ever sees, but is That Portion of The Creator called the Soul.

Children throughout the world are not being instructed properly on the Gift of human life. There is so little understanding on the Purpose that human life was created for. Everything is humanistic and, many times, the humanistic practices are not pure; in fact, they please only the enemy of The Beloved Creator, and also all human life.

Today as I speak, there are Many Here with Me, because it is so important that human beings of all ages, backgrounds, degrees of understanding, and also abilities too numerous to mention, open their minds to the fact that *human beings of all backgrounds have a Goal, and that is to one day return a Portion of themselves, the Soul, to The Creator of All Things.*

Though the Soul is not something that is seen with the human eye, but It is obviously present in the mind of a human being, because though a human being speaks openly, acts openly, there is always something within them that allows them to know if what they are doing, saying, is right or wrong for some Portion of them within them; not just their mind, but Something Deeper than that. We hear some call It *conscience*. Perhaps this word is close to what the human mind can perceive that inward feeling to be held, reminding them of the importance of what they say, do, think, or are example of.

So much has been delivered through this Gift of The Father's Love, because of the importance of human life. Remember this: When harm comes to the physical body, it is oftentimes very serious; a hand, a leg, an eye, or many other situations that cause an individual to not be able to use all the faculties they've got to live a normal life. But this Miracle has been given to mankind of all degrees of intellect, all backgrounds, a Great Lesson on the ***Importance of That Unseen Portion that Exists in human life, called the 'Soul'. It is the Connecting Link to The Creator, and It is That Portion of human life that each human being is responsible for.***

I smile when I say My next Words: You would not cut your finger off just to see it bleed; you automatically protect your physical. The next time you find yourself having an impure thought, act, deed, remember, it affects your Soul, it cuts your Soul off from being pure, and it saddens The Creator, because do not forget, your Soul is a Portion of Him. ***This you must always remember.***"

JANUARY 30, 2002 AT 12:50 P.M.

## OUR HEAVENLY MOTHER

"**I** am your Heavenly Mother.

The Father, in His Love for human life, has given a Blessing beyond what any human mind can perceive It to be. Perhaps you have heard Me speak these Words before. They are Important Words, because They are to awaken the minds of all age groups of human life that The Father's Existence is Real, and all things from human life are seen.

When a man, woman or child receives a gift that pleases them, it shows in some way, some form, some degree. I say these Words with much Love for human life, but I also say to human life that The Father, in His Love for the Souls of all human beings, has delivered, and is delivering, a Gift Greater than any mind can perceive.

The Father, in allowing So Many Saints Here to speak, is to awaken the minds of all degrees of intellect of the Closeness human life has to The Divine, but also revealing to human life that once these Saints walked the earth, and are now Blessed to the Degree of Sainthood for the Soul They bore during life as a human being.

This Gift that bears the Name of The Beloved Saint Joseph, is a Gift enlightening all minds to the Importance of What Saint Joseph stood for when He walked the earth as the Foster Father of The Son of The Creator. Logic says He was not ordinary. Now, today in your time, He walks the world through one voice, and All of the Heavens teach human beings of all degrees of intellect, the Importance of How Close The Divine is to them, through the Words Each One speaks.

One small voice was chosen to deliver millions of Words. Logically, this would be impossible for the human mind. Do not forget this statement of Mine.

I would like to add one important statement. Children are not being instructed on the True Presence that they are exposed to every day they breathe, they act, they participate in the human way. So little is being instructed by those who feel they have the knowledge, the power, the interest, the ability to teach on what is called spiritual subjects, but in many ways the human side enters, and it is not as this Gift is, because All Here in the Heavens speak directly, wanting Their Words to be put into script so there can be no misconception of what is meant.

The Souls of every living human being are Portions of The Creator, unseen but obvious in many ways, especially when an individual has to choose purity over impurity, love over hate, truth over untruth, and many more things, that in the human way, each human being is subjected to every day.

As I close My Words with you, I beseech you to remember, to be born as a human being is a Blessing that nothing else has the privilege to be."

JANUARY 31, 2002 AT 1:00 P.M.

### SAINT ALPHONSUS LIGUORI
### SAINT BENEDICT
### SAINT GREGORY THE GREAT

There are three Saints Here: Saint Alphonsus Liguori, Saint Benedict, and Saint Gregory The Great.

"**F**or thousands of years human life has been blessed with a Goal. The Goal is beyond what the human mind can fully comprehend, *but men, women and children should see the human mind as a Gift of Divine Love.*

In the beginning of human life, human life had to be taught many, many things through experience, and through learning, by doing, by living the human way. All things were done in stages, helping this creation of human life to develop into what The Father Willed it to be: understanding, intelligent, and able to make decisions regarding their lives, their way of life, and many other things.

At this time in which I speak now, human life has come a long way. There were different times in the history of human life that during the learning stage of so much that was available, individuals sometimes found it difficult to use all the senses they had, all the abilities, because a learning stage, in many ways, has steps to it that must be taken one at a time, helping the individual to increase in the knowledge, the ability, the concept, the reason, the purpose, the way. All these words mean something, because this is how human life came about, to the degree it is, in your day.

You live in a time not just of material progress, but a time wherein the human mind has the ability to judge what is pure over impure, right over wrong, just over unjust, truth over untruth; also, the value of all things that are created and, also, all things that are developed through the minds of many human beings.

My Words were to prepare you for what I am about to say. It is *innate* in human beings to have a goal. Some chose it more strongly than others, but there is a very important part in choosing a goal, and that would be *logic* in the *value* of the goal.

Throughout the world learning is an important factor; learning about many things. Understanding is an important factor; that is, to be able to judge what is right over what is wrong, what is pure over what is impure, what is correct over what is incorrect, what is helpful over what is perhaps dangerous. With all this background of human life easily adapted by just living, should automatically tell all men, women and children that ***human life was created for a Purpose, a Goal, a Reason Designed by a Higher Entity of Being.***

**I**t is important, All that has been delivered through this Gift of Divine Love be passed throughout the world, because there is so little understanding of what a Precious Gift human life is to everyone who receives it; not just a few, but everyone. *Human life has a Goal for a Portion of it called the 'Soul', the 'Connecting Link of Divine Love' that is innately felt, never seen, but logic to every human being, because of the innate desire to reach goals.*

**H**ours, days, years, could be spoken on this subject alone because, do not forget, in the beginning of human life all who were born learned one thing at a time, and that was to survive in the human way. They were given the ability to understand they had to eat, they had to make sounds to attract others of their kind.

**S**o much has been given since that time, because of every human being *being Gifted with a Portion of The Creator called the 'Soul'.* If this were not true, human life would be like all other living things, with no judgment, no sense of logic, and no desire to learn more; but, human life with this Precious Gift of being born this way, must understand that *there is a Goal for a Portion of every living human being born, and It's called the 'Soul'. It is the Greatest Gift of Divine Love, because It has a Higher Place to Exist In than ever before.* So be it."

FEBRUARY 1, 2002 AT 1:03 P.M.


### SAINT ALPHONSUS LIGUORI

"**I** am Saint Alphonsus Liguori.

**E**ach time the world of human life becomes so degrading in morals, values, intentions, understanding of why they were created, *The Father's Will comes forth through some individual, The Father using a force not understandable to human life, but able for human life to handle.*

**T**he world you live in is truly worse than the time so oftenly spoken about as *Sodom and Gomorrah.* These Words are spoken in a light manner. They should be spoken in a very forceful way.

**C**hildren are not being instructed on the full meaning of the Commandments of The Creator, because the Commandments have been diminished into such a concise format, supposedly making them easier to learn, but in truth this was only an excuse by many who partook in this project.

**M**ost children are more alert to what is morally good than they are given credit for, but if they are in the company of those who speak, supposedly, in a more educated way, it makes things sound so practical and natural to the human determinations of their meaning. Children are being subjected every day to immorality in an in-depth form that is not seen as being vile to the Souls of all who partake in it, or who demonstrate through their actions, their so-called freedom to do what they will, they wish to do.

So Many Saints Here in the Heavens find this time in which you live *a time of evil interpretation*, thus causing much injustice to the Souls of millions of human beings. We hear some say, 'A picture is worth a thousand words.' All of Us Here in the Heavens question this remark, because it means so little and yet it causes many to think impurely in many ways.

*The Father, in giving to the world this Blessing that is so obviously a Blessing, because of All that is delivered, enlightening human minds to the importance of being a human being, and the responsibilities that are important for the whole way of life, for the Goal intended for the Soul that is to one day return to The Father, The Creator, The Giver of life, bearing the Name 'Saint'.*

As I close My Words, I close Them with a firmness with which I spoke. *Human beings of all ages must stop ignoring the Gift of human life, for the Perfect Goal The Father Intended for the Soul of every human life, and that was to return to Him in Glory, bearing the Name 'Saint'.*"

FEBRUARY 2, 2002 AT 11:08 A.M.

"It is innate in human beings to reach
for goals of progress — for needs and for help
on important issues.

It must be constantly a reminder to all
ages of life, that human life was created to
reach the Goal appointed by The Creator, and
that is to return one's Soul to Him at a given
time; thus, in doing this, it closes the
Connecting Link that occurred at the moment
of birth — the body and the Soul. The Soul,
through the body, is returned to from Where
It came, a Blessing, a Gift of Divine Love
that nothing else has."

FEBRUARY 4, 2002 AT 1:06 P.M.

## THE SACRED HEART

"**I** am called The Sacred Heart of Jesus. I have heard individuals question this Name in ways they could not understand a Child being the Heart of the One in whom It was born.

So many times words that are a little different are misunderstood, only because those who hear the words are not capable of understanding the value, the importance of what the words mean. Sometimes it is purely a physical meaning, but when it is connected to The Divine, it is associated with The Divine Will of The Creator, the Personal Love of The Creator, and also the importance of what was created, especially when it is a human life, because in the human way there is a Goal Greater than men, women and children understand the Goal to be. It is a Goal for That Portion of them that is a Portion of The Creator known by the name 'Soul'.

So much has been delivered on the importance of human life, and its Close Association, Connection to The Divine. When We hear a question, or I should say a questioning of how this can be, We ask the individual to think that the lineage of human life, in its importance, began

with The Divine, for a Goal to return to
The Divine and be called 'Saint'.

The Father has given to the world a
Gift of Words, instilling into the minds
of millions of human beings the
importance of being a human being, the
reason that is instilled in a human being,
that there is a Goal beyond what is
understandable to the human mind, but
is obviously a point of reality.

So many hours could be spoken on
this Close Association that human life
has with The Holy Trinity. It is
important that children understand that
they have a Future, a Goal, a Purpose, a
Reason for their being born, because
without this there would be no reason
for the Rules of human life to even exist.

Animals live differently. Each one
has a purpose, but none have the
mentality, or the ability, or the reason
for life that a human being is Gifted
with.

As I leave you, I beseech you,
cherish your way of life, and remember,
in your senses, in your abilities, you
have been given the Gifts to fulfill the
Goal you were created for, and that is to
return to The Father a Portion of you
that you cannot see, but through your
logic in what is pure over what is
impure, what is truth over what is
untruth, there is within your mentality

an understanding of the importance of what you have the mentality to understand.

And as I close My Words with you, I remind you, purity of the mind and body is what your Soul absorbs in everything you say, you practice, you partake in, you believe in, and you do."

FEBRUARY 5, 2002 AT 12:55 P.M.


## SAINT ALPHONSUS LIGUORI

"**I** am Saint Alphonsus Liguori.

**T**here are several of Us standing together. Souls oftentimes do this. We All smile, and many times We are very interested in conversations to those who are with life yet, and who are discussing matters, conditions, how man would say 'pro and con'.

**W**e Saints are closer to human life than anyone can perceive it to be, for through the Souls of human life, Our Presence is easily part of the conditions, the situations, and what is being practiced or is occurring. True, We do not shout 'Stop' when We know it is evil; it is not the way The Father designed Our Way to be.

**I**t is sad when I say the next Words. So many learned men, women, and even children, cannot perceive that *human creation has a Goal, and when what man calls 'death' comes and the human life can no longer act, think or use the faculties of human life, there is a Remaining Part of that human life, the Soul.*

**S**o many times We hear, 'I need help.' The issue can be many things, because men, women and children, through their human minds, often seek help for what is occurring or what they are thinking to do, to practice, or to stop others on some act or condition that they cannot agree with.

**I** speak differently today, because you do live in a time that every day is turmoil to millions of human beings. Sometimes the turmoil is the inability to see justice over injustice, right over wrong on simple things, hope over despair, on issues that are beyond what the human mind is capable of being able to evaluate the situation, to the degree where it can be more comfortable, more understandable, more reasonable, and sometimes even more reliable than the first thoughts on it, or about it, were evident to the mind.

***Human life is a privileged creation of The Father's Love, because it has a Purpose, a Goal,*** and it also has many attributes, giving it the strength to exist in the human way; also, giving it the courage to stand up for what is right, what is proper, what is moral, what is just, even though many times, in decisions, many individuals do not evaluate the conditions properly, and do not behave in a justifiable manner.

Let us now take the mentality of a thousand individuals of all backgrounds, and every one is told a very important fact. Ask yourself: Will everyone look at the fact, and see it in the context of its greatest value, or its personal value, or its strength, giving hope, more understanding, and giving to life the ability to realize that this one thing could make them a Saint? *Rarely is the Goal of life thought about when decisions are requested to be made.*

I know I speak differently at this time, but there will be some who read My Words and it will suit their life, their situation, their mentality, and hopefully will give them the strength to inwardly be able to fulfill what is necessary in a justifiable way, and in a way pleasing to the Soul that is much a part of human life, thus pleasing The Father in a Divine Way.

My Words are different, but the love for human life by All of Us Here in the Heavens never diminishes, never dwindles, because We, too, walked the road of human decisions, human priorities, human involvements, and many human mistakes.

*As I close My Words, there are Many Here with Me, and Each of Us wants all Souls to be returned to The Father, Saints. It is not an impossibility, it is truly a possibility. In human life it is natural for individuals to seek goals. The Greatest Goal any human being can achieve is to one day become a Saint."*

FEBRUARY 6, 2002 AT 12:47 P.M.

## SAINT ATHANASIUS

**"I** am Saint Athanasius.

It is sad for me to say heresies are prevalent throughout the world. *A heresy is demeaning to all that is pure, correct, just, and right.*

So many individuals find heresies challenging and, in some ways interesting, thus ignoring their own inability to understand logically that the heresy is against what is valuable to them, to their mentality, *and definitely to their Soul.*

Throughout the world today there are thousands, even millions of living human beings who, each day, use human life as a necessity for physical things and so-called practical things, but ignore the sound reasoning for the gift of understanding morality, because of the Soul they are the custodian of.

So Many Saints have spoken, in so many ways, understandable to millions of human beings, and yet, it is so easy for so many to accept what is *obviously against* what is valuable to their morality, and to their mortality.

Today as I speak, I speak with deep love for human life, because All of Us Saints Here in the Heavens want human beings of all degrees of background, intellect, abilities, to realize that the physical body ends at a point in life, *but each life is carried on through the Soul they were given at the moment of their conception, and their Soul is the Living Part of the creation that is Close to The Creator.*

Many, many men and women instruct others on their interpretation of what life is all about.  So much of it is only their interpretation, and not realistic to the Importance of the Purpose for which human life was created, and also, That Portion in each human life that is a Gift of Divine Love, namely the Soul.

I could speak endlessly on this subject, but the Points I have just given you are important for you to fully understand that *you, as a living human being, are responsible for a Portion within you that is not part of man.  It is Part of The Creator that will return to Him according to how you lived at your time, and I say to you now:  Be aware of all these Words; They are Words of Concern, Hope and Love.*"

FEBRUARY 7, 2002 AT 1:27 P.M.

SAINT ATHANASIUS

"**I** am Saint Athanasius.

**W**hen my name first became evident to thousands of people who did not know anything about me, All that was spoken at the time my name was announced was news; it was encouraging to many individuals who felt the need for what I stood for.

*Today as I speak, I speak with much love and gratitude to The Father, allowing me to be a Part of this Great Gift of His Divine Love for the Souls of millions of human beings, that have no concept in knowledge that they are the custodian of a Soul of Such Greatness, and also, the fact that this Soul, at one time, is to represent them in Heaven.*

**S**o many places throughout the world there is so little understanding of the Importance for which human life was created, and very little understanding that there is a Goal for the Soul of every human being.

**C**hildren are not being instructed on why it is important for them to not do unkind things, or have impure thoughts. Most parents do not explain that there is a Goal for life, and that all that a human being does in the human way, the individual is accountable for one day.

*Sometimes a child feels so much closer to The Divine when he or she learns that they were created for a Goal, a Place to go, for a Portion of them that will never end, and it is important because at that time they will be Close to The Creator they have learned about, they have been instructed on.*

Another thing a child, and even older men, women and children should learn about the Goal of life. It is not being instructed by those who feel they have the learning, the knowledge to do it, because oftentimes the human part of life becomes more evident, and then the spiritual part of life is not seen for the Importance of it, the Importance of acknowledging the True Existence that it stands for in the lives of every human being.

All of Us Saints Here in the Heavens cherish this Miracle The Father has given, because *it is Our sharing that gives Hope that more Souls will be saved, for the Purpose for which They were given at a particular time, to an individual who knew nothing about The Divine.* Ask yourself: Would it not be sad not to have a Goal for life? Would it not be hopeless in daily living not to feel that you were living for something to give you and your way of life Purpose?

As I close My Words at this time, always remember, through this Gift of The Father's Love that so Many of Us Saints have had the privilege to speak through, *you too, one day can become a Saint, and become a Part of helping others to more fully understand what a privilege it is to be born as a human being, with a mentality, a will, and yes, the understanding that there is a Goal to life nothing else has."*

FEBRUARY 8, 2002 AT 1:12 P.M.


### SAINT ALPHONSUS LIGUORI

"**I** am Saint Alphonsus Liguori.

**E**verything that has been delivered verbally and in script, through this Gift of The Father's Love for human life, must be scattered throughout the world.  There are millions of Souls waiting for It to arrive, because of the Knowledge, the Inspiration, the Logic, and the Divine Love that these Gifts of The Father's Love express, through so many Saints instructing constantly on what a precious gift human life is to an individual human being.

**C**hildren are not hearing the Words, nor are They being spoken to them in Their full context.  The next Words are sadness to me.  All that has been delivered through this Gift of The Father's Love is being held in abeyance by those who once had a deep, sincere feeling toward what the gift of life fully meant.

**A**ll of the Saints Here in the Heavens speak through this Gift, even when They do not announce Their Names.  Many times it appears as casual talk, or on a subject matter that draws attention.

**T**he world is in total chaos, emotionally, mentally, spiritually, *because so much* *emphasis has been placed on humanism, rather than Who created human life.*

As I close My Words, I will add one statement: All the Saints Here in the Heavens ask The Father to help, in some way, to instruct those who are in the human way, *that they have a Portion of Him within them that they live with every day. It is a Gift of The Father's Love, because It gives strength to every part of a human being's nature, character, mentality, and will.*

I close and I say: *There is no time that The Father does not listen, or be aware of what an individual says, participates in, or acts upon.* So be it."

FEBRUARY 11, 2002 AT 1:27 P.M.

## SAINT ROBERT BELLARMINE

"**I** am Saint Robert Bellarmine.

The small voice The Father uses to repeat Our Words to you, is to encourage all of human life to see the Goal for which human life was created, *this Goal being to be returned to The Creator in purity.*

*The whole world is laden with diabolical sources, forces, conditions, and meaning, because the enemy of The Creator of All Things wants to be seen, to be followed.* It is not jealousy, it is more than jealousy, because such demonic pleasure is definitely weakness in many ways, and the only strength that shows is to conquer some of the Souls of human beings, that basically should be one day returned to The Father, Saints.

*It is not a battle between The Creator and evil. The Creator is in Control,* but through the gift to human life *to be able to choose* what an individual wants to do, to say, to feel, to express, to own or to be in charge of, allows *the free will* the ability to make decisions.

The Father has given to the world a Gift beyond what the human minds of millions of human beings can fully comprehend. He has allowed one voice, one body, to be used to deliver Information and Direction so that human life of all degrees of intellect would have the advantage of choice, and not just domination to choose what is pleasing to The Father, and what is best for their Soul.

So many of Us Saints speak through this Gift of Divine Love, and We truly understand that through some Words, the way in which They are spoken are easy for some individuals to comprehend in a deeper degree, the importance of the meaning; and then, other Words are spoken, and the reception of Them, the consideration in Them and, of course, the understanding of what They mean, helps other individuals, through their mentality, to discern a greater degree of what is meant for them to understand the advisability and the importance to look at the conditions, the circumstances that they are exposed to daily, and use their logic and, of course, their love for The Creator, in how they commit their allegiance, their affections, their interests, their way of life to what they see as not just a normal reaction, but a reaction that is fulfilling to the Soul that they are the custodian of.

*As I close My Words I bless you with The Father's Love, and His Will that, in your understanding of All that has been delivered thus far by so many Saints Here*

*in the Heavens, you will find in your way
of life an in-depth love for having become
created a human being, because of the
Soul and the Goal you are Blessed with."*

FEBRUARY 12, 2002 AT 12:43 P.M.

SAINT JOSAPHAT

"**I** am Saint Josaphat.

**T**o speak today and have My Words put into script, is a privilege beyond what I can say. All the Saints Here in the Heavens are eager to please The Creator, The Father, in every way. When He beckons to One of Us that We must speak, it is an act of Divine Love Our Way.

**M**en, women and children throughout the world need to read so they can more fully understand what a Beautiful Gift The Father has given to man. *So many Saints have been requested to speak through this Gift of The Father's Love, in Honor of The Beloved Saint Joseph. It is important that everyone who reads What has been delivered, understand that there has never been so much Divine Direction through one voice, for such a length of time, since the time The Son of The Father walked the earth.*

**Y**ou live in a time of great importance, because The Father, in seeing all that is going on that is detrimental to Souls of millions of individuals, took a stand and said, *'We must not leave all who are born to the world alone at this time.' That is why this Gift of His Divine Love was given through The*

*Beloved Saint Joseph, for all ages of human life to more fully recognize the Value of what human life has been Gifted with, and that is a Portion of The Creator, namely the Soul.*

We hear so many say, 'I cannot see It, I cannot feel It.' Through your mentality, and through the senses in your being, you are aware of the Closeness you have to Something you cannot see, but you, through your understanding of what is pure over what is impure, what is just over what is unjust, you innately know you have responsibilities to never ignore, in your decisions, what is morally correct over what is immoral, what is unjustifiable over what is justifiable.

I could dictate millions of Words on this subject. All of Heaven is united through The Father's Will, to instruct not just verbally, but allowing It to be put in script so millions of men, women and children cannot say they never heard of the Closeness human life is to The Creator, and the Importance of it every day, in every way.

Needless to say, *All of the Saints Here in the Heavens want this Gift of the Father's Love, bearing the Name of The Holy Spirit of God, to help Souls become Great Saints.*

As I close My Words, I say with much love to you who write these Words, and who will read these Words, 'Human love is something many human beings cherish and depend upon in many ways, ***but Divine Love is Above all that a human mind can comprehend such an Ultimate Gift, because The Father, in His Own Way, wants the Soul that is a Portion of Him to be returned to Him in Purity, in the manner in which He Gave It at the moment of conception.'***

**I** beseech you, remember these Words. They will give you strength at times when it is needed."

FEBRUARY 13, 2002 AT 12:45 P.M.

SAINT AGNES

"**I** am Saint Agnes.

**I**t was, and is, a privilege for me to speak through this Gift of Divine Love, and have My Words put into script, hopefully for millions of all ages of human life to read What The Father requested I say.

**H**uman life is of the Utmost Importance, because it bears within it a Portion of God Himself. This Portion receives all that the individual practices, participates in, instigates or does. *So many young people should be instructed that when they think they are alone, they are not alone. They have a Portion of God Himself within them; It's called the Soul.*

**S**ometimes a little one becomes frightened, thinking all they need is a physical body to give them security. *Remind them that they are never truly alone, because within them The One Who created them is with them.*

**T**hroughout the world there is such a great need for human life of all ages to understand more of their Close Connection to The Creator, and their Personal Association that they were given at the moment of their conception. Human life was created because The Father, in His Love for this creation of

His, added to it a Portion of Himself, Unseen, Unheard, but obviously within, helping a human life to more fully understand that there is a Creator of All Things. There had to be, because no human being could have created all things.

*The world has been given this Beautiful Gift of The Father's Love, having so Many Saints Here in the Heavens speak to all ages who are alive, and most of them named after a Saint.* Be aware of all you think, you say, you do, and the importance of how others, in their imitation of you, in their communication with you, in their understanding of you, can help them more fully understand that there is a *Goal to human life*. It is not called *man*, it is called *Sainthood*.

*I am so happy to be able to speak these Words on this day, because All of the Saints Here in the Heavens want this Gift of Divine Love to spread throughout the world in all languages, so that millions of Souls will be saved.*

As I leave you, I want you to be reassured, it is The Father's Will that I have spoken, and to me it is a Gift of His Divine Love to do this."

FEBRUARY 14, 2002 AT 12:52 P.M.

## SAINT JOSEPH, THE HOLY SPIRIT

"I am Saint Joseph.

It is important that All that is being delivered through one voice travel throughout the world. Much will have to be translated in languages understandable to other cultures, other intellects, others' manner of living.

My Statement is Very Important, because there are millions of men, women and children who need to know about this Gift of Divine Love, and also need to know that The Father, in giving this Gift to the world, wants all cultures and all Denominations of Faith to be able to see the Beauty in It, and the Value It is to their whole being.

Children are not being instructed properly — in many cases, it is too time-consuming to those around these children — the importance of understanding that human life is gifted with a Portion of The Creator, not able to be seen but logically felt, because of the innate sensitivity to what is right over what is wrong, what is truth over what is untruth, what is good over what is evil.

All that has been delivered through this Gift must never cease, because throughout the world there are millions of human beings who are unable to find where they can learn specific facts about human life that their culture, their background, is incapable of helping them to know.

So much has been given in an orderly way through a small number of individuals who have been given the responsibilities to see that what is occurring in a special place, a specific place, regarding the importance of human life, and that human life was created for a Goal.

The very fact that human beings of all ages, all backgrounds, innately feel that something they do, they say, they act upon, has a goal to it that makes this goal satisfying or gives strength, in some way, some manner, some degree, to themselves or to others, logic speaks here, and reminds all who read these Words that human life was designed and created for a Goal. Naturally, the body is used to absorb all that is needed to arrive at the Goal for the Soul that each human being is gifted with.

The responsibility of this statement should be obvious to all ages, all cultures, all natures, all degrees of intellect, for every Word spoken that The

Father decrees to be, there is a positive Goal for It, Reason for It, because human life bears within it a Portion of The Creator.

I smile when I make the next statement. In the human way, there is an innate protectiveness for those who are loved, those who are cared for. This tells all of human life that The Creator of All Things also instilled this sensitivity, reminding human beings of all ages, all backgrounds, that there is more than they sometimes think about to their responsibilities in how they respond, and what example they are, because human life has a Goal for a Portion of it, called the Soul. The Soul, as a Portion of The Creator, is a Gift beyond what any other thing a human being can possess or achieve.

I close My Words and I say, 'The Father, in His Love for human life, has given human life a Precious Goal.'"

FEBRUARY 15, 2002 AT 12:55 P.M.

### SAINT BERNADETTE

"**I am Saint Bernadette.**

There are so few books being read reminding men, women and children of the Importance of Sainthood.

You live in a world of little discipline, and little understanding of what is sound morally, what is acceptable morally. All ages have succumbed to being active in what they feel pleases them at the moment; very little discernment on what the action will cause them to do if it becomes improper, impure, at a particular time.

If you were to ask one hundred people at this moment, strangers that is, if they could tell you what the Commandments of The Creator were all about, you would find much injustice in their response, even some vulgarity.

So many people of all ages, all backgrounds have adjusted to what is acceptable, rather than what is morally sound and correct. Excuses have multiplied in so many ways. Some individuals have an improper idea of what happiness is, what morality is, and what life was created for. Humanism is based on what is pleasing for the moment, or how an individual physically feels.

So many Saints have spoken through this Gift of The Father's Love for human life. There is nothing or no one throughout the world, that all ages have not been given the in-depth meaning of why they were created, and what The Father expects of them.

So many men, even some women, feel they have the intellect to be judgmental on what is moral, what is immoral. Basically it is mostly their opinion, and this opinion could be based on their own laxness in obedience to the Commandments The Father gave for all of mankind to have the Rules to live by.

*WHEN THE COMMANDMENTS WERE FIRST DELIVERED, THEY WERE NOT IN THE CONCISE MANNER THEY ARE LEARNED AT THIS TIME. WHEN THEY WERE DELIVERED, EVERY FACET OF LIFE WAS INCLUDED IN WHAT WAS MORALLY RIGHT, PURE, SOUND, CORRECT, AND IT IS SAD FOR ME TO SAY THAT TIME HAS ERASED THE FULL MEASURE OF WHAT THE COMMANDMENTS ARE ALL ABOUT.*

Needless to say, volumes could be written on not just the Beauty of the Commandments, but the necessity for them to be understood. Many Souls have suffered, because the ones in whom They were placed ignored even the conciseness of the Commandments, thus being too eager to look indepthly in their action, their thoughts, and their association with other human beings.

Hundreds of books could be written on the full meaning of the Commandments that were given to assure human beings of all degrees of life, of mentality, that the Rules The Creator gave were of Great Importance to every facet of life. When We hear an individual say, 'I feel I am living a good life,' many times the individual is innately accepting many immoral weaknesses.

*THE FATHER HAS GIVEN TO THE WORLD A MIRACLE OF INSTRUCTION THAT MUST NEVER BE SET ASIDE. EVERY VOLUME THAT A SAINT SPEAKS IN GIVES STRENGTH, WHETHER IT IS FELT IMMEDIATELY OR NOT, BUT THE SOUND FACTS IN WHAT IS SPOKEN TO BE READ AND FOLLOWED, ARE SO OBVIOUSLY LOGICAL, FACTUAL, AND HAVE A DIRECTIVE IN THEM FOR ALL DEGREES OF INTELLECT, ALL AGES OF MEN, WOMEN AND CHILDREN AND, YES, ALL THE DIFFERENT SO-CALLED FAITHS IN THE CREATOR THAT WERE ADOPTED BY SOME INDIVIDUAL, FEELING HE OR EVEN SHE, HAD THE POWER, THE KNOWLEDGE, THE ABILITY, TO INSTRUCT ON WHAT IS*

## *CORRECT IN HUMAN BEHAVIOR, FOR THE GOOD OF ONE'S SOUL.*

As I close My Words, I must add one statement. Never think you are alone, you are not. Your Soul is ever present wherever you are, whatever you are doing, even when you are sleeping."

FEBRUARY 18, 2002 AT 12:53 P.M.

## OUR HEAVENLY FATHER

"I am your Heavenly Father.

The time in which you live is a time of great sadness in many ways, because there are so many definitions for what is pure over what is impure, what is just over what is unjust, what is valid over what is invalid, what is acceptable over what is unacceptable.

The world has been blessed, in many ways, by what has occurred in the past years through this Gift of The Father's Love, the Divine Love of The Creator, for men, women and children of all ages to be able to see the value in what is logical in being a human being, over what would be illogical if you were a human being acting as an animal.

We smile through this little one, because Our Words are difficult to repeat.

The world has been blessed by this Gift of Divine Love in which, through which, so much is being instructed that no human mind could fully describe. The value of being a human being is beyond human understanding, because human life is a Gift of Divine Love. So many individuals do not see it this way, because they do not understand all the Gifts that human life has been endowed with since its first creation.

Human life has abilities to fully understand morality over immorality; also, the beauty of a pure love over an impure desire to love. Impurities lessen the value of everything they touch.

We hear some individuals say they have been disgraced by the impure actions of others they know. They could have avoided the disgrace by not participating, but it is so natural to blame others for one's own inabilities to stand up for what is morally sound over what is temptation, or participation.

There is so much to be spoken on this subject a thousand volumes would not cover, because the volumes would have to go indepthly on each Commandment, beginning from the very first one to the last. Just as an example, I will use the fourth one, 'Honor Thy Father And Thy Mother'. Is not this Commandment applicable to each person involved, and how many parents break this Commandment in a multitude of ways, thus not being proper example to their children?

I could speak hours on this subject, because it is a subject of great need, not just at this time in which you live, but has been since the beginning of the creation of human life.

As I close My Words, please know, All the Saints in the Heavens want this Miracle of The Father's Love to be spread throughout the world, because there is so much deep love and sincerity expressed through It by so Many Here in the Heavens, and so much Importance is placed on the Soul that every human being is Gifted with, plus always encouraging all degrees of mentalities to more fully understand that they are the custodian of a Portion of The Creator that is to be returned to Him in Purity.

I could speak hours on this subject, but oftentimes it is important for those who read the Words to not be overwhelmed by the amount, but see the Value and the Degree of Divine Love that can be spoken in fewer Words."

FEBRUARY 19, 2002 AT 12:35 P.M.

SAINT ATHANASIUS

"**I** am Saint Athanasius.

**H**eresy is not a thing of the past; it is openly present at the present time, and has been for a great length of time.

**I**t is sad for me to say that belief in a Creator is oftentimes expressed in the same tone that belief in an ordinary thing is liked or disliked. There is very little distinction in how an individual uses his or her mentality in a casual, indifferent, impractical, lackadaisical attitude, manner, whenever the subject of Sainthood arises, or even Higher than this — The Father Who created All Things is mentioned.

**T**housands upon thousands of Words have been dictated in several of the past years on the importance of human life, and its Close Association with The Holy Trinity, with The Divine, with The Creator of All Things. *There is so much sadness sometimes, Here in the Heavens, when We hear so little respect regarding the Importance of the Goal for which human life was created; granted, not the body, but that Inner Portion, the Soul.*

**I**t is sad to have this ignored, because so much emphasis is placed on the flesh and all that the flesh contains, forming the body, giving to the body the ability to think, to feel, to be active, and to be able to learn so many things on so many subjects.

When We hear an individual make claim to want to follow in the footsteps of others who took the responsibility to represent The Divine through a formal organization, it is sad for All of Us to see so much desecration, and vile acceptance of the duties attached to this occupation of human life.

All of Heaven speaks through this Gift of Divine Love, and most of the Subjects are pointed to enlightening individuals on what is expected of them, what they should follow mentally, morally, physically, because of the Soul they are the custodian of, *and the Soul, as a Portion of The Creator, though It is not seen, is obviously felt through a mentality, or through the senses, when one is making a decision on what action to take. Should it be vile, contemptible, and lack any sign of purity, or will anyone care that they are responsible for every action they perform, they partake in, as a human being?*

They say there's a Goal to life. Then is it not a logical responsibility that a goal immediately says 'accomplishment', but it also says it takes a certain innate ability, effort, understanding, and a sense of justice to accomplish the end result when it is a Goal that gives Greatness to the body and, of course, to the Soul.

I could speak hours on this subject, it is of such great importance, because as I speak at this moment, what is occurring in many places would make you vomit at how vile and contemptible the actions are. The physical is a Gift from The Creator, the mental also, and all the abilities of human life have a reason, a purpose. *It is more logical to choose acts of loyalty to The Creator* than disrespect, or ignore totally what a *Great Beautiful Gift human life is*, and it has a *Goal* that nothing else created has.

I know as some read these Words they will be shocked at the straightforwardness, but I assure you, throughout the world there is so little human respect for human life, all ages, all backgrounds.

*The Father, in His Love for human life, is using His Holy Spirit to deliver verbally and in script, Something for all ages of human life to read and more fully understand that human life is in Divine Plan, because it has within it a Gift that nothing else has. It's called a Soul, a Portion of The Creator that is to be returned to Him, and be able to be called a Saint."*

FEBRUARY 20, 2002 AT 12:54 P.M.

SEVERAL SAINTS

"**T**here are Several of Us present at this time. We hold the little one tightly, because of the Power that Our Presence causes on her body.

*The Father has given to the world a Gift Far Greater than the human mind can perceive It to be. He uses one voice, one intellect, one source, to speak What He Wills to be delivered from Him, and from All the Saints Here in the Heavens.*

What has thus far been delivered must travel throughout the world, and very soon. Idolatry of all that is wrong is evident in every area of mankind's life, practices, intentions, and decisions. Man calls it 'humanism', acting as though the word 'humanism' can give more credence to what is occurring.

We hear some say, 'All that has been delivered through one voice, is difficult to travel to other languages.' This, of course, is excuse. *Excuse is prevalent throughout the world. There are excuses for everything that is diabolical, everything that is practiced, thus ignoring the Commandments that were given a long time ago.* True, the Commandments were made more concise than They were given at another time, but so many excuses are being humanly justified, *but not spiritually accepted or acceptable.*

Men, women and children, most times, in saying prayers, say them much faster, with very little meaning than they would be said if they were ordering something materialistic, humanistic.

The world has been blessed with so much encouragement to see the value of human life, *the Importance of the Soul of human life and, of course, the Reason for this Gift of The Father's Love for human life,* allowing so Many Here in the Heavens to instruct in Logical Formation, Format, the importance of human behavior, and how it should be handled.

All ages are resisting and rejecting this Gift of Divine Love; excuses are boundless. It is important that All that has thus far been delivered, and will be delivered, be passed throughout the world, irregardless of whether They are acceptable or not, because it is important that you understand that *at this time in the history of human life, The Father, in His Love for this creation, the importance of this creation, because it bears a Portion of Him, wants human life to battle the enemy that is obviously present every hour of the day and night.*

When children are corrected, there is very little explanation; also, there is very little understanding in all ages of human life that there is a Greater Source, Force, than what human beings understand life to be, ***and it is necessary that this Miracle of The Father's Love, bearing the Name of The Holy Spirit of The Creator of All Things, be spread in every direction possible, because 'daily' the evil that exists is a greater distraction than anyone sees it to be.***

I have used so much power through a small body at this time, because the Warning is Important. It is not a 'suggestion', and you who read this must understand the Words that are being easily thought about, saying, 'You live in a time worse than Sodom and Gomorrah,' it is an excuse comparing the true picture of what is occurring.

Thousands of Words could be put into script on the importance of human life, and the importance of human life understanding indepthly that responsibilities are multiple to this creation of The Father's Love, ***because within this creation He has always, and continues to do it, and that is to put a Portion of Himself, Unseen, but obviously there.***

***The Word is the 'Soul'. Return It to Him in the Beauty and the Thanksgiving for which He entrusted It to you, for It to one day be able to be called 'Saint'."***

FEBRUARY 21, 2002 AT 11:54 A.M.

## GOD THE FATHER

"Mankind — human life must understand that I cannot be replaced or misplaced.

The Importance of All I Desire must be understood as being Important to human life and that Portion of it that I Am.

The world must know of this Miracle of My Love that is being given at this time, to awaken all of human life of My True Existence and My Purpose for My Creation of Human Life.

There is a Portion of Me in each human being. It is not seen but is logically felt, because each human being is aware of what is a pure act over an impure act. Also, that in My Gift, My Presentation of My Commandments, I have released so much Logical Information on what is Important for human life to live by, because of the Goal for the Soul that exists in each human being born.

The Soul, as a Portion of Me, gives to human life a 'UNION OF LIFE' nothing else has.

**I will speak more at another time on this Important Relationship all of human life has with Me."**

FEBRUARY 21, 2002 AT 12:48 P.M.

## SAINT THERESE OF LISIEUX

"**I** am Saint Therese of Lisieux.

*The Father has given to the world a Gift of His Divine Love, beyond what a human mind can fully perceive the Magnitude of this Gift.*

So much is taken for granted, and so much is put into a natural, informative understanding. Humanism, materialism and cooperation, when it is not for the best of the morality of all concerned, or for the good of the morality of all concerned, is taken for granted as being a natural act of human life. Justification abounds throughout the world on whether something is moral when it is totally immoral and, of course, the list is endless on this subject.

In this Gift that The Father has given to the whole world, it is sad for me to say that it will be a long time before this Gift is presented to other lands, other places where It is desperately needed. The human mind instinctively knows what is beneficial to whatever subject that is the point that is being spoken about, whether it be spirituality, morality, or the close relationships that people have with each other.

I speak on different subjects, because human life has been gifted with various ways to express, to partake, to divulge, to enlighten, ***and to be example of What The Father Wills for the Souls that each human being communicates with through their association with the physical portion of life.***

**M**y Words are different, but it must be understood that human life, in so many ways, ignores what a Precious Gift it is. Human beings refer to the cultures, the mentalities, the backgrounds, and many other facets that each human being encounters in their association with other individuals.

**I** speak differently today, but as We watch every day, human beings of all backgrounds, all goals, all talents, and all personalities, ***We try very hard to get them to use their free will, or I should say, so-called 'free will' in a beneficial manner for the sake of their Soul, that they are the custodian of, responsible for, and will be the Only Portion of them at a later date.***

**P**erhaps what I have spoken, some who read the Words will say, 'I am confused.' There is nothing confusing about what I have spoken. It is to alert all of human life, all ages, to be aware that all the gifts of human life have a purpose, a reason, but so many times an individual prefers to ignore what they know is right, and follow what they see others partake in, practice, or promote.

**I** could speak hours on the importance of the importance of the mentality of human life, but also, the responsibilities, due to the fact that every human being is born with the understanding of knowing what is right over what is wrong, what is truth over what is untruth, what is just over what is unjust; and also, that human life is different than any other living matter or thing, *in that human life has a Goal that nothing else created has, and that is for the Soul to return to The Father, bearing the name of the individual in whom It was placed, but the Goal is Far Greater than the human mind can perceive greatness to be.*

**A**s I close My Words, I know I have spoken differently, but hopefully some of the points that I dictated will give strength in areas that are needed, to give an individual the ability to more fully understand *there is a Divine Plan in human life. It is The Father's Will for this to be understood, never ignored. There is a Goal Higher than the human mind can perceive a goal to be.*"

FEBRUARY 22, 2002 AT 12:39 P.M.

### SAINT IRENAEUS

"**I** am Saint Irenaeus.

There are multiple reasons for this Gift of The Father's Love for all of mankind. I smile when I say, 'Saints from all different areas have been chosen to give the Words They are Instructed to give, for the benefit of Souls from all backgrounds of life.'

**O**ftentimes, when a particular Saint Here in the Heavens speaks, the very fact that the Saint is from a particular area in the world gives strength to someone, or even many, who read the Words that the Saint delivers, and they feel a warmth, a closeness that sometimes is indescribable.

*The world has been blessed by The Father's Love for His Creation, human life.* All that has been put into script thus far must be passed throughout the world, because It will give strength in areas, ways, that are too numerous to mention, *because human beings need to know that Sainthood is a Reality and a Goal.*

Children are not being instructed properly on the importance of how they live their life, and that their habits, their wills, must always do what is morally correct and pleasing to The Creator, plus pleasing to All the Saints, *because Sainthood in its very*

*Existence, helps many individuals become stronger, morally, mentally, physically, spiritually,* many times even when They are not known by the individuals that They are personally helping, and supporting their goodness, *because logic says that the very State of Sainthood wants All Souls to become Saints.*

The Father's Will is Important, and men, women and children should innately know that human life has a Goal. The Purpose for which human life was created, was of Great Importance, and is of Great Importance, *because it is through the Father's Will Sharing What He Is, Who He Is, with the Souls that will be returned to Him, bearing the name of an individual who walked the human role.*

So much could be spoken on this subject, but I close My Words with one thought for you: *There is no greater goal in life that you can reach than Sainthood, through your will, your love, in wanting to share the Beauty and the Presence of The Beloved Holy Trinity, that awaits All Souls to be returned from Where They came."*

FEBRUARY 25, 2002 AT 12:31 P.M.

"The Heavenly King, in the beginning of creation of human life, put Portions of Himself in specific places, Three in number; that is why the Words 'HOLY TRINITY' mean Much More than They are read to be.

In what is known as 'The Holy Family', this was a Special Gift of Divine Love, for all of human life to follow, would see the Importance of family life, and the reason for which family life was so important to the future of all life.

Today there is so little emphasis on the dignity, the importance, and the sound spiritual background for which human life, and family life, were designed. Children are not being instructed on the sound reality for which they were created, and that The Creator of All Things Designed the creation of human life, and the Goal for human life.

Men, women and children refer much to personalities, natures, characteristics, knowledge, and the communication that human life is capable of with others like themselves, and also, through prayer with The Divine.

Today this Beautiful Lesson is to
encourage all mentalities of human life
that they were created by Divine Plan,
and their way of life has a Purpose, and
definitely a Goal, because in the design
of human life, The Father instilled a
Portion of Himself, and still does; It's
called the Soul.

Needless to say, What I have just
spoken is for all ages, all backgrounds,
all degrees of intellect, to realize that
their life, their human life, has Divine
Plan, and they should understand that as
they desire in the human way to profit,
whether it be in friendship or just
association with others, but by 'profit' I
mean a close relationship of honor,
dignity, understanding, giving to each
life a happiness, because of the
knowledge they can share, or the
abilities they can share, and also, other
gifts of human life that help each one
involved, because each one can relate to
it being a human association,
understandable because of it being so
closely connected in all the senses, all
the abilities, and in the mental abilities
that differ, and yet give strength in
many areas of human life.

I close My Words at this time, but
not without saying: Human life is the
most blessed Gift of Divine Love, over
and above all other living matter or
things. I also add to this: The Father, in

**giving this Blessing of human life, instilled in it many, many Gifts that He felt would encourage human life with interest and hope."**

FEBRUARY 26, 2002 AT 12:46 P.M.

SAINT ATHANASIUS

"**I** am Saint Athanasius.

**T**hroughout the world, in all countries throughout the world, there are many heretical practices in many areas of how mankind lives, thinks, and uses for benefits they feel necessary, but where heresy is concerned, there is much doubt by those who understand how wrong heresy is, so they should not participate or accommodate those who practice this way of life.

**T**hroughout the world there are so many heretical practices by those who say they believe in what Christianity is all about; also, that they are very authoritative on the reality of it, the worth of it, and what it can be used for, beneficially used for.

**C**hildren are not being instructed on the importance of morality, and that this particular practice can destroy them when it is immoral in concept, content, and many other facets of how a human being thinks, and uses other things, other people.

**T**oday as I speak, if I were to put into words the ugliness of how, what, many individuals of supposedly high standards of living, or who have the mentality greater than others, use so much diabolical suggestions, practices, ignoring totally that *they were* *created by A Divine Entity of Design, Value, Truths, and Love.*

I close My Words, because What I am saying in between the Words that have sound to Them, is too difficult for the little one We All use, to handle the sight of so much desecration to the morality of millions of human beings throughout the world. Very little is ever spoken about the wrongs, the impurities, the vile contemptible practices that are not just degrading to human life, but to the Souls of human beings.

I will close My Words, but as I do, What has been spoken is not just for those who put the Words in script, but for those in faraway places. Hopefully it will awaken their minds to more fully understand that *human life was created by The Divine, for a Goal to return to The Divine in the Sainthood Role.*"

FEBRUARY 27, 2002 AT 12:38 P.M.


## OUR HEAVENLY MOTHER

"**I am your Heavenly Mother.**

In the creation of human life, The Father gifted it with many gifts that, through time, have developed in many areas available to more understanding, more knowledge and, of course, more abilities to value what is important over what is unimportant.

Human life has been blessed with what man calls *'progress'*. Progress covers many areas of development, of ingenuity, and in being able to intellectually understand more about many things. The human life is also like a barometer. Each individual senses it differently than others. There is no degree of intellect in any human life that can fully perceive or understand the Magnitude of The Creator, and His Divine Plan.

You live in a time of great importance, in that all ages of life are capable of accomplishing difficult situations, more abilities to do things that at other times they were not able to do. There are no two mentalities exactly alike. If this were so, human life would become discouraged because of the

oneness that all people would feel at a
given time.

I speak differently today, because
it is important that this Miracle of
Divine Love be seen and read throughout
the world, by all mentalities, all age
groups, all backgrounds of human life.
The Father, in His Love for human life,
gives to human life many Lessons
directly, and indirectly, on the
Importance of Why He created human
life.

The physical part is very
important, the mental part supports the
physical part, but there is another
Portion within human life that is rarely,
if ever, spoken about, and very seldom is
there a consciousness of It, and that is
the Soul that every human being is
Gifted with at the moment of conception.

The mentality of human life has the
ability to progress, and address many
subjects. The physical part of human
life is gifted with many physical
abilities, giving more energy to human
life, and the ability to do many things
with the physical that, without it, an
individual would have no way to use the
limbs, or the mind.

I know What I speak is different,
but it is important, because men, women
and children rarely, if ever, think of
what a Tremendous Degree of Divine

Love Designed human life, instilling in it
Gifts beyond what any other species of
life has. Also, it is important that this
Gift of The Father's Love be spread
throughout the world, irregardless of
any rejection from any authority, or any
specific area of knowledge, that claims
to know more than this Gift speaks
about, Instructs on, because this Gift of
Divine Love, human life, has a Goal.

Since the beginning of this
creation, The Father has instilled much
knowledge, much interest, many
abilities, but also, more understanding
regarding the creation of human life,
and that it has a Purpose and a Goal
beyond what any other creation has.

As We Instruct through one small
voice, the Script that is put forth at this
time is of the Greatest Importance to all
of human life, present and that to come.
It is reasonable that All that The Father
has delivered through this Gift, *bearing
the Name of The Beloved Holy Spirit of
Him, called Saint Joseph,* is a Gift to be
seen for the Greatness It is, the Divine
Love in It, and the Purpose for which It
was created.

Today is a day that should be a
beginning to help millions more fully
understand that The Father, in His Love
for human life, is making human life
aware that they have the responsibility

to stand for what is important for That Portion of human life that is a Portion of The Creator of human life.

I add to this: This Gift of Divine Love does not have a complicated name to remember, because the word 'Soul' is easy for all degrees of intellect, and all ages, to say and to remember. The Father, in His Divine Love, uses this short word so It cannot be forgotten. Remember these Words; They are given with much Love, much Sincerity, and much Hope."

FEBRUARY 28, 2002 AT 12:49 P.M.

SAINT STANISLAUS

"**I** am Saint Stanislaus.

It is a privilege for me, as a Saint, to be able to be a Part of this Gift of The Father's Love, wherein so many Saints have had the privilege to dictate Words of Enlightenment, encouraging all ages of human life, all denominations, to become aware of The Divine. In reality, it should be an automatic understanding that there has to be a Divine Power, because of all that life has been given, in so many ways, for so many reasons.

Today as I speak, it is important that throughout the world there should be a constant reminding of the *Truth, the Beauty, the Logic, in understanding the True Existence of a Divine Creator.* Throughout the world there is so much emphasis on using the human body instead of the human mind, for direction, for courage, for strength, for hope, and for a future.

Children, at this time throughout the world, are subjected to what is standard in certain areas, for them to learn all about life. In so many ways the reasoning is confusing, but also, not truly based on the Importance of What human life is gifted with, and that is *a Soul, a Portion of The Creator that basically is the Main Strength, Source, that all human beings have, to help them more fully understand that human life was created, as man, for a Higher Goal, to one day return to The Father, a Saint.*

*All of the Saints Here in the Heavens take part in this Gift The Father has so Lovingly given at this time, with so much Instruction, Reasoning, Purpose, giving to human life a Higher Goal than anything else created.*

Today as I speak, it is sad for me to say, there are thousands, multi-thousands of human beings, at this moment ignoring the gifts of human life, and they are pleasing only the enemy of The Creator, and of human life.

*Prayer is an Important Part of daily living,* but it is passed over by millions every day, because of preoccupation, which is thought to be important to the way of life, thus ignoring that *it does not take a lot of effort to keep some type of communication with The Divine, thus giving more strength to one's own habits, abilities, and care for what is occurring that is diabolical in many phases of it.*

I close My Words, but as I do I must say to you, the voice I use is a 'Victim Soul' that no one fully understands, because there are so many distractions that human life is part of in the daily way. *Through this Miracle that*

*bears the Name of The Beloved Saint
Joseph, more Divine Love has been given
than any time in the history of human
life except, of course, at the time The Son
of The Creator walked the earth,
appearing human, not Divine."*

FEBRUARY 28, 2002 AT 1:21 P.M.

SAINT BENEDICT

"**I** am Saint Benedict.

The Father has given to the world a Blessing through thousands and thousands of Words. *The Words contain Instruction, Teaching, and have a Purpose to Them that must be seen for the Worth It is to the human minds of all people*, not just those who feel they have learned as much as they can handle regarding what life is all about in its spiritual content and abilities.

Today as I talk through one voice, it is important that All that has been delivered through The Father's Love for mankind never be held hidden from the world. *The world must be saturated with All the Script or so-called Written Words that contain so much Instruction, Direction, Concern, Hope, for the Souls of millions upon millions of human lives, present now and those to come.*

The Books that have thus far been put into Script are for the future minds of millions of human beings, as well as being useful for the present time. *Nothing is to ever stop Them from being put into print and passed throughout the world, no matter what language an individual speaks;* it is The Father's Will at this time in the history of human life, that So Much has been delivered for the benefits of millions of Souls yet to be born to the world.

   Yes, I said, 'Souls born to the world'.  I hear some say, 'Only the physical is born.'  As each new physical is born to the world, a Portion of The Creator is instilled, not understandable to the human mind, but Important for the individual in whom the Soul is placed.  The Soul is a *Strength* in many areas of what a human being is all about, and yet the Soul is the *recipient* of all that a human being practices physically, verbally, morally.

   I close My Words with My Sincere Desire to give strength to anyone reading these Words because, in many ways, it is a Command of Direction to be carried out for the benefit of millions of Souls."

MARCH 1, 2002 AT 1:25 P.M.

## OUR HEAVENLY MOTHER

"I am your Heavenly Mother.

This Gift of Divine Love that The Father has given to the world, is a Gift of Instruction to all human beings, encouraging them to more fully understand that human life has a Plan.

Today everyone throughout the world will have different thoughts, different ambitions, different ideas, and different attitudes on many things. Human life was created with a gift such as this is.

Children are not being instructed on the importance of morality over immorality in every issue of life. We hear adults say to children, 'That was bad, why aren't you good?' but there is little reason attached to the definition of what is good, what is bad, thus the individual not understanding what is truly acceptable.

It is important that this Gift of The Father's Love is seen throughout the world, and what I am about to say will surprise many people. It is to be seen through pictures that show who the instrument is, and some of the things that have previously occurred, because to read the Written Words does not emphasize the full picture of What this Gift is all about.

Thousands and thousands and thousands of Words have been delivered in an Instructive Formula, for thousands of individuals to understand the meaning of What the Message or Messages meant.

It is so easy for men, women and children to read something, but then either forget it, or not fully understand the full meaning of what the words meant for them, to not just read, but to keep within their mentality the importance of the meaning, because perhaps the words will give them more awareness of a situation, an occurrence, or a personal problem that might arise.

I speak differently today, but then do not forget, All that is delivered through this Gift of Divine Love is for hundreds or even thousands of different mentalities, different degrees of understanding, different personalities, different backgrounds, and different living conditions that so many people ignore, rather than see the in-depthness of what they are associated with, or part of, in actions, in attitude, in participation, or in behavior.

I could speak hours on this subject, because to be created a human being is a Gift of Divine Love, and through one's personality, nature, character, there are so many diversifications of understanding what certain things mean for them personally.

Many Blessings have passed through this Gift, mostly in instruction on the importance of life, and that life in the human way has many responsibilities, but also, many gifts. One without the other would not give to human life the beauty of understanding, the beauty of being able to discern the challenges that give to human life, strength, hope, satisfaction, and goals.

I bless you for writing My Words, but I also say, 'Do not forget, the Gift of human life has a Goal.' So be it."

MARCH 4, 2002 AT 1:02 P.M.

SAINT CLARE

"**I** am Saint Clare. I have rarely spoken openly through this Gift of Divine Love in which The Father constantly shows His Divine Love through so many of the Saints Here in the Heavens.

So many times We hear individuals question: 'What is Heaven? What could It be like? There are no bodies There. Do the Souls recognize Each Other by name?' We All smile at this because the human way of thinking is very evident. Even when individuals talk to The Creator of All Things, most times they only picture a human form, *but He is Much More than this.* The beauty of human life was given by the Ultimate Source of Communication that only The Divine has recourse to, and also control of.

Though it is difficult for many individuals of all ages to think about what The Creator looks like, Where He Exists, We All smile at this, because human beings of all ages automatically associate The Divine with the human figure and mind. That is why it is so important that all degrees of intellects, all backgrounds of life, begin to understand that *the Soul that is given at the moment of conception, is beyond what the human mind can comprehend, but the Soul is constantly aware of all that the individual does.*

I smile when I say My Next Words, because the Soul oftentimes feels They are in care of the one in whom They were placed at the moment of conception.

As a family grows, there are always those who are in charge. This tradition has been handed down through time, so it is logical to say, for each birth of a human life, The Divine is involved and, of course, *the Soul of every individual innately understands and knows that They are Part of The Divine, and in Their efforts to help those in whom They are placed, They try very hard to get the individual to see the nature of the importance of purity of the body and the mind.*

I close My Words now, but as I close Them, I want to add: The Father's Love for human life is Far Beyond what a human mind can compare their way of love, their way of understanding, to exist. So be it."

MARCH 5, 2002 AT 12:50 P.M.

### SAINT CATHERINE OF SIENA

"**I** am Saint Catherine of Siena.

**I** am surrounded by many Saints as I speak to you today, and Each One of Them wants Me to say Words of encouragement regarding how you approach what is moral, what is sound, what is pure, what is just, because many times, when it is done in a frivolous way, it causes much harm to the minds and the Souls of those who are present, and see your act of disrespect, lack of concern, regarding the dignity that Sainthood should receive.

*All the Saints want this Gift of The Father's Love, called 'The Miracle of Saint Joseph', to spread to all languages, all backgrounds, all intellects, and all degrees of spiritual understanding.* Throughout the world at this time, in so many ways, and so many places, sound spiritual recognition, concern and practice is being eliminated, and it is sad to see so much sinfulness by all ages of human beings.

**W**e hear some mention that they have read the Bible, but they also add, 'That was for another time.' Perhaps what occurred was at another time, but the Messages within the Words reveal the importance of how human beings should use their senses, their abilities, for what is pure over what is impure, for what is just over what is unjust, what is pleasing to The Father over what is vile and contemptible, morally, mentally, physically.

**As I speak, the Power We must use through one small body is a Power beyond human understanding.** She listens throughout a full day, not for the rustle of Our garments, but for Our Presence that she has been trained to recognize in a particular way.

I hold her tightly, and I show her a scene. There are three men, three women. She is watching their actions. Their actions are obscene. She says, 'Cast them aside, I cannot bear it.'

Thousands of men, women and children express themselves in so many ways, totally indifferent to what is morally pure, sound, acceptable. They ignore totally what harm they are doing to the ones they are abusing in many ways.

We show her another scene. Children are playing in a yard. She is happy with this scene, but suddenly now she cries, because evil has entered the scene. We will draw it away, because she could not handle what could have happened at a time when children are the evil's prey.

As I close My Words, be assured that you do live in a time of confusion based on immorality, and a lack of concern for what is morally sound, pure, correct. **That is why** *this Gift of Divine Love has been given to the world, and instructed to be put into script, because without the script the Words would fade away, and never be remembered.*

All that has been delivered thus far must travel throughout the world, irregardless of the language barrier that oftentimes is used as an excuse when certain individuals do not want to read what they are capable of reading, especially when they find it opposite of what they are doing.

You live in a time of so many indiscretions, so much carelessness in morals, and very little concern over the full and true meaning of purity of the mind, the body, for the Soul.

I will close My Words, because the little one has been tortured by what I have shown her. *Every moment of the day, be mindful that you were created for a Beautiful Goal for your Soul, and as each day is important to you now, through your Soul you will live in a manner and way that will give you a happiness inconceivable to your mentality now, but at the time that it occurs you will thank The Father for having learned about the Goal you were alerted to be able to have for your Soul."*

MARCH 6, 2002 AT 12:50 P.M.

### SAINT STANISLAUS

"**I** am Saint Stanislaus.

The Father, The Creator, The Almighty, has given to the world a Gift of Divine Love, incomprehensible to the human minds, of the Magnitude they are allowed to partake in: the Magnitude of Love, Purpose, and Association.

At this time in which you live, *The Father wants all degrees of intellects to see, to understand, to realize, that to be born in the human way, called man, is truly a Gift of Divine Love.* The way of human life is greater than human beings understand it to be, not just with the Gifts instilled into human life, but the Goal for which it is destined to be.

Too few men, women and children attach a Goal to human life other than the ones that they mentally feel, or they are involved in physically, emotionally, in the human way. *The Portion of life that is rarely thought about is That Portion of Divine Love instilled into all human life; It's called the Soul.*

Even though all ages of men, women and children use the wording, 'We are soul mates,' they do not see the fullness of the statement, because they are only looking at it and sensing it to be a close relationship, boundless for human needs, association, and closeness to another human being.

Today as I speak Words, perhaps familiar in some ways, but the Words are to be seen for the Importance They are to every human being.

*In the creation of human life The Father designed it to one day be returned to Him, after having allowed it to walk in a path of humanistic values, understanding, conditions, thus allowing the Soul of the individual to earn a place with The Creator, giving to the Soul the ability to more fully understand the privilege of their place, representing a human life through the works and the Words of the Divine Love, so beautifully expressed in How The Father, Why The Father created man.*

There is so much importance to human life, to every individual born in this form, this degree, this way. Too little is understood regarding the Purpose for this creation of Divine Love. *It was The Father's Way to share All He Is, because of the Magnitude of What He Is.*

Thousands of Words could be spoken on this subject. Some already have been at different times, but hopefully those who read these Words today, and others who will read Them, will find in the Words a Closeness to The Creator, that nothing else can truly help them understand what a privilege it is to be born as man.

**W**e All smile when a Lesson of this degree is given, because We know at the time it is given only a small number of individuals will read It, and feel the Importance of It, but the Importance of the Written Words will go through time, enlightening others of the Importance of the human association with The Divine.

**A**s I bless you with The Father's Love, I ask you to remember each day, before you lay your head to rest, say: *'Thank You, Father, for this day, and that You created me for a time to come that my Soul will return to You, bearing the Name Saint.'*

MARCH 7, 2002 AT 12:58 P.M.

SAINT CLARE

"The little one The Father has chosen for this monumental task, is driven by a Force of Divine Purpose, Reason, Reasoning, and Divine Love.

The world has been blessed with a Gift of this dimension. *The obvious Truths that pour forth through this Gift of Divine Love, are intended to lead not thousands, but millions of Souls to The Father at a given time.*

The human mind is a Gift beyond any other living matter or thing, and it is through the human mind that all degrees of mentalities, all backgrounds of human life will see the Importance of All that is, and has been delivered for a very long time.

As We listen to those standing on the outside of this place where you are, many of them believe without question, and sincerely want to spread What is being delivered, because of the Logic in It, the Purpose in It, and that it is beyond human ability to speak how a Saint would speak, to think how a Saint would think, because do not forget, *you are not dealing with the human side of the Saints, you are dealing with Their Souls, and Everything that is delivered is as The Father Wills It to be, because this*

*Gift of Divine Love is to give to all of human life available, the importance of human life, and that it has a Goal different, but One beyond what a human being could possibly imagine the Beauty of, or the Magnitude of, because it is through the Soul that Sainthood is made possible for a human being.*

There are many, many theologians throughout the world who have read, and continue to read theory on what human life is all about. *The Father has given this Gift, bearing the Name of The Beloved Saint Joseph, and in this Gift so many Saints have been requested to speak, instructing as They go, to all degrees of intelligence, the Importance of human life having a Soul, and the Importance of the Soul, because It is That Portion of human life that will return to The Father.*

Today as I speak, I say, 'There is no Saint Here in the Heavens that does not want to see every human being alive not know about this Gift of The Father's Love that expresses openly, clearly, the importance of human life that no other living matter or thing is the custodian of.'

We hear so much emphasis on the pride that is taken on the mentalities of several individuals that openly are talked about. It is important that more emphasis be put on the Soul that is rarely spoken about, because It cannot be seen, cannot be heard, but It is definitely felt in a natural form, way, condition, that causes a human being to know that what they are doing is either right or wrong, good or evil, pure or impure.

The Father has given to the world a Gift Greater than the human mind can comprehend It to be, because as He has requested so many of Us Here in the Heavens to partake in this Gift to human beings of all degrees of values, concerns, and all other human things, the world has been blessed.

The time has come that this Gift of Divine Love cover every corner of the world. It is needed, because there are no other words put into script that give so much information on what human life is Gifted with.

As I close My Words I bless you, those who write the Words, and I beseech you to remember: *There are millions of Souls that want these Words, and All the other Words that have been given, to be heard by those with whom They are a Portion of, but cannot be seen, felt, or acknowledged, because the Soul is a Hidden Gift of Divine Love by The Creator of All Things.*"

MARCH 8, 2002 AT 12:43 P.M.

SAINT ATHANASIUS

"**I** am Saint Athanasius.

**T**here are Several of Us present, because of the Importance of the Subject Matter. The world is in chaos. There is so much immorality that the average living human being does not take the time to determine if an act or speech or situation is moral or immoral.

**T**here are so many individuals walking in weakness, yet feeling they are walking in a modern way, a way expected because of the time in which they live. *Throughout the world, each day, there are so many sins practiced against the Commandments of The Creator. When the Commandments were given to Moses, each Commandment was dictated in much detail. Through time, human life has a way of shortening the Words, feeling that time is more necessary than the Words could mean.*

**C**hildren are not being instructed on the importance of their intellect, why they have it, and the purpose for which it was created. The laxness in instructing all ages is not just a sadness to see, but in some cases devastating, because it is harmful to the Souls every day.

When a human being gets killed,
murdered, the injustice is felt in many
degrees. I am not saying that it should not be
felt, but sometimes the very same people who
feel that way about the physical, ignore the
spiritual necessity in life, and the reason for
it, because humanism seems to supersede
what life was created for, and that human life
bears a Gift of Divine Love that should be
protected at all costs, *because as It is a
Portion of The Creator, Its Purity is the
most Important Fact of anyone's nature,
performance, involvements,
understanding and/or educational aims.*

I speak differently today, because there
is so little thought in the human minds that,
each day, every individual of all ages does not
deal with just the material or the social facts
of life; they deal with the Soul that they are
entrusted with at the moment of conception.
The Soul is the *recipient* of everything they
do, think and say.

Maybe the comparison I can give you,
will help you to understand what I have just
spoken. You see an article, and you do not
know what the article is, but yet you take
chances out of curiosity, and you handle the
article because of your curiosity. The article
is poison to your system, or even to your
mind, and yet you do not question the in-
depth reasoning regarding this article.

Every day of your life you are handed an article, whether it be words, direction, conversation, or physical communication. I say to you on this day, think of the situation as the importance of it, and how it will involve you, what it will cause you to react to, respond to, relent to, or be a victim of.

I know My Words are different, and perhaps some who take Them or read Them, will not feel or see or understand, that every day of human life every individual born must look at the day as a time closer to, hopefully, use it to become a Saint; not an impossible idea, but practical in every way.

I close My Words with a Blessing because, you see, in the human way there are so many things in life that look practical, necessary, but remember, if you have one question, say a prayer to yourself, *and the Best Prayer you can say is: In Nomine Patris, et Filii, et Spiritus Sancti. Amen.*"

MARCH 11, 2002 AT 12:55 P.M.

### SAINT JOHN OF THE CROSS

"**I** am Saint John of The Cross. My Title is important to me because it tells things about me that life, as it is now, should know; also, should know about many other Saints Here in the Heavens Who walked the human role. In many ways Sainthood is ignored, because the human mind cannot sense, commit, understand, or put into words, the Reality of the Goal for which human life was created.

**C**hildren are not being instructed on the necessity of prayer. Many only connect prayer to a time when they are in a special type of service, but other than that, they never think of *prayer as being, or should be, a daily practice of communication with The Creator, The Father Himself, or some Saint Here in the Heavens.*

**M**y next Words are sad for me to say: You do live in a time of much immorality, and many individuals walk in despair, not hope, because so much is placed on materialism, humanism, and the practices so many are involved in, that are immoral.

**T**oday as I speak, it is to encourage all who take My Words and who will read My Words. Ask yourself: Is it not logical to have a Goal for your life when the living part of you no longer exists?  Also, ask yourself:  Is it not true that as each day opens to another day for you, is it not a day of activity, responsibilities, and hopefully, enjoyment in a moral role?

My Words today are important for many to read, as All that passes through this Gift are for different individuals of natures that need to think about; also, amazing personalities that can entertain others by their very presence.  There are many gifts to human life, not all recognized for the worth they are.  Everything becomes so commonplace and, in many ways, habit.

Children are not being instructed on the importance of each day of their life, the privileges they automatically have, and others that they encounter by their actions. Morality is not spoken about.  Purity of the mind is not spoken about.  Obedience to the Commandments of God are not spoken about. Throughout the world there is much confusion, because of the lack of sound belief in The Creator of All Things.

*The Father's Love for human life is beyond what a human love can be, but it is necessary for all ages to understand that human life is a Gift of Divine Love, and has a Goal to it.*

As I close My Words with you at this time, I remind you of one thing:  You, as an individual, have responsibilities in everything you do, you say, because many who see you do not realize that they imitate how you think, what you think, and also, they are impressed by how you look to them. Every human being is example to others every day of their life. It is important to remember this because, do not forget, *The Father, in His Love for human life, put a Son upon the earth as Example. The list is endless in how He showed Example, and at another time, I will talk about this.*"

MARCH 13, 2002 AT 1:08 P.M.

### SAINT JOHN OF THE CROSS

"**I** am Saint John of The Cross.

The Father, in His Love for human life, has many times given to men, women and children, another individual to instruct them on the importance of human life, and the manner in which they should follow to reach the Goal that awaits them.

There are many, many discontented human beings throughout the world. Very often the discontent is based on their lack of importance to others, their lack of sensitivity to others, their lack of knowledge about what others feel, think, say, practice.

*In this Gift that bears the Name of The Beloved Saint Joseph, much has been addressed to all ages of life regarding the importance of life, and the Goal that it was created to reach.* The Father chose one small voice, not a loud voice, because a small voice will be heard easily with no strain to it, no dominance in it, but a perseverance that was necessary for those to listen to, and to better understand the beauty of having been born as man.

Throughout the world there is so little sound, truthful direction. So much of the direction is based on human opinion, human sensitivities, and human importance.

**I** will not speak long at this time, because What I have said is for all to read, and look at the Words in Their Meaning, and adapt the Full Meaning to their way of life, protecting themselves in many ways.

*As I leave you, I bless you with The Father's Will, because it is His Will that will one day pronounce Judgment on how you lived your daily way."*

MARCH 14, 2002 AT 12:53 P.M.

SAINT CHRYSOSTOM

"**I** am Saint Chrysostom.

**W**e All smile when the little one The Father has chosen for this Gift of His Divine Love, as she announces Our Name to those present, she oftentimes hesitates to be sure that she heard correctly. She does not hear with the sound of her ears. What We speak is an Implantation into her mental, and she repeats Our Words as They are decreed to be, because They are Important Words, and not natural to be spoken by human beings.

**T**he world has been blessed abundantly through this Gift of Divine Love. There are thousands, there are millions of men, women and children that should be told about this Gift to them through one voice, *because of the Importance of the Instructions, the Directions, and the Purpose for which this Gift has been given, for all of mankind to more fully understand that they were created by The Divine for a Goal, for a Portion within them that will represent them at a given time. It is called a Soul.*

**W**e hear so many individuals use the words 'soul mates' when they feel close to someone else; they feel an independence and a security. Every human being born, through their Soul, is Connected to The Creator of All Things; It is a Connection not obvious, but always there. So many Words could be given on the Closeness human life has with The Divine. It is not a mystery, it is fact.

At this moment there are a great number of children being born throughout the world. ***Each one of them is gifted with a Portion of The Divine.*** Sorry to say, thousands of them will not be trained to understand that their life is important, because they have a Portion within them that is different than any other living matter or thing has. It is a Portion of The Creator, called the Soul.

In the so-called religious schools throughout the world, there is very little instructed on ***What human life is Gifted with, the Importance of It, and that It is a Living Part that will return to The Heavenly Father after the physical of the one in whom It was given no longer exists.***

We hear many individuals get angry when they hear someone lie about something. Sometimes they even become violent because the lie was intimidating on some subject, or it caused a situation to be discussed, clarified, due to the fact that the lie covered something important to them.

In the beginning of human life many stages had to take place. It was important to The Father to do it this way, because of the importance of human life.

You live in a time of many heresies; also, much is occurring that is thought to be justifiable, because an individual feels that the situation is wrong for them to have, or them to be victims of.

Needless to say, volumes of books could be written on this subject, *but It Is Important, this Gift of The Father's Love for human life, because It bears the Name of The Beloved Saint Joseph, and as He was The Foster Father of The Son of The Creator, He has once again come to the earth, prepared to give Strength, Hope, Endurance, Love, Direction, and He uses many, many Saints to speak, helping those who write the Words, and those who will read the Words, to more fully understand that to be born as a human being is a Gift of Divine Plan.*

As I close My Words, I bless you who write Them, and all who will read Them, *because it is Important for the Souls of millions of human beings to be returned to The Father to one day be with Him Forever and Ever. Amen."*

MARCH 15, 2002 AT 12:38 P.M.

## SAINT ANTHONY OF PADUA

"**I** am Saint Anthony of Padua.

**H**uman life does not like to be the victim of anyone's anger or sense of humor.

**I**t is important that this Miracle of The Father's Love be passed throughout the world in every way possible for it to occur.

**W**hen, through this Gift, it is said, 'You live in a time worse than Sodom and Gomorrah,' many who read this statement reject it, and they feel that the time they live is only a time of progress with great learning abilities.

**C**hildren throughout the world are not being instructed on what is morally correct. It is sad for me to say that, most times, *the word 'moral' is only said or concerned with the human feeling towards morality and immorality, totally ignoring what it does to the Soul, because men, women and children cannot fathom that they have a Portion within them that is also a Portion of The Creator of All Things.*

**W**e hear some say: 'If this is so, then why do I have so many problems? Why am I not perfect? Why do I not understand all the important things that take place? And when I read, would not my Soul help me better understand subject matter that I have never learned about, never thought about, never been subjected to?'

You live in a time wherein human life resists so many important facts, because it is easier to remember how one associates with one's surroundings, one's associations, one's mental abilities.

The Father does not say, to walk in a pure way you should have been born in a different way, with different parents. The Father does say, 'You have been given a will, you have been given understanding of what is right over what is wrong, what is good over what is evil, what is just over what is unjust; ignoring this knowledge does not make it go away.'

Needless to say, *All of the Saints Here in the Heavens want so much for this Gift of The Father's Love for human life, to reach millions of men, women and children, awakening their mentalities to more fully understand that they were created for a Reason, a Goal Greater than any goal they can humanly understand.*

As I leave you at this time, I beseech you to deliver All that has been thus far given through this Gift of Divine Love, to the whole world of human life, no matter what language they speak. Remember one thing, as you head a piece of paper with the Name of a Saint, it will attract attention to Something that is Good, and has Something Important to say.

*As I leave you, I bless you with The Father's Love, and with The Heavenly Mother's desire that all you partake in through this Gift of Divine Love, one day you will see accountable to your name, your service to The Divine that you practiced, participated in, in a loving way."*

MARCH 19, 2002 AT 12:45 P.M.

## OUR HEAVENLY FATHER

"**I** am your Heavenly Father.  I will speak quickly.

I have given to the world, the whole world, a Gift of My Divine Love, bearing the Name of The Beloved Joseph Who, in reality, was the Foster Father of My Son when My Son walked the earth.

Through this Miracle of My Love that bears the Name of The Beloved Holy Spirit, humanly called 'Saint Joseph', it is sad when I hear individuals doubt that I would speak at this time.  It is important that All that has been delivered be passed throughout the world, but handled with dignity, honor and sincerity.

As the world has been blessed by so many Messages, pertaining to how I expect human life to perceive the Importance of human life, and Why I created it, placing within it a Portion of Me, though this may be difficult for some to understand, nonetheless, it is factual in My Divine Plan.

Though it is difficult for some to say, to think, to feel, to understand, that so much has been passed through one small voice for the sake of millions of Souls in human lives, it is My Will It be recognized for the Value It is, and the Divine Love that it took, that it takes, that is in What I have given, throughout the world, so that human beings of all backgrounds will have the opportunity to understand My True Existence and, also, that within each human life I place a Portion of Me.

In so many areas throughout the world you live on, mankind feels it is important to be skeptical that I would speak at this time. It is only sadness for their Souls, and to the Souls, because humanism does not have the abilities to fully understand the Importance of Why I created man and, of course, the word is 'mankind' when it covers all of human life.

Today as I speak, I speak not with anger, but an In-depth Sensitivity, because throughout the world, this Miracle must be known for All It Is, because It is My Gift to human life, to instruct them on the Importance of Why I created human life, and What Portion of human life is a Portion of Me, of Who I Am, What I Am.

I will not speak longer, for My Power through this little one is Above and Beyond what the human mind or body would be capable of enduring for too long a length of time. My Words, All that have been spoken before this time, are to be spread throughout the world, whether They are rejected or lied about.

Remember My Words."

# INDEX

**GOD THE FATHER**  4, 78, 90, 122, 124, 125, 185, 194, 243

**OUR HEAVENLY MOTHER**  14, 19, 34, 43, 54, 70, 84, 87, 116, 148, 206, 215

**THE SACRED HEART**  157

**OUR LORD**  49

**SAINT JOSEPH, THE HOLY SPIRIT**  80, 105, 178

**SAINT AGNES**  93, 176

**SAINT ALPHONSUS LIGUORI**  13, 108, 110, 133, 151, 154, 160, 168

**SAINT ANGELA MERICI**  100

**SAINT ANTHONY OF PADUA**  240

**SAINT ATHANASIUS**  6, 9, 28, 38, 51, 102, 119, 143, 163, 165, 188, 204, 229

**SAINT BENEDICT**  151, 213

**SAINT BERNADETTE**  181

**SAINT CATHERINE OF SIENA**  30, 60, 68, 130, 220

**SAINT CHRYSOSTOM**  237

**SAINT CLARE**  218, 226

**SAINT DOMINIC** 1, 113

**SAINT FRANCIS OF ASSISI** 95

**SAINT GREGORY THE GREAT** 151

**SAINT IGNATIUS LOYOLA** 72, 127

**SAINT IRENAEUS** 63, 199

**SAINT JOHN OF THE CROSS** 65, 232, 235

**SAINT JOSAPHAT** 173

**SAINT JUSTIN MARTYR** 46

**SAINT MARGARET MARY ALACOQUE** 57

**PADRE PIO** 123

**SAINT PATRICK** 136

**SAINT PEREGRINE** 24, 138

**SAINT ROBERT BELLARMINE** 145, 170

**SAINT STANISLAUS** 210, 223

**SAINT TERESA OF AVILA** 75, 98

**SAINT THERESE OF LISIEUX** 17, 196

**SAINT(S) UNNAMED** 41, 56, 141, 156, 191, 201